PERFECT ENGLISH Style

PERFECT ENGLISH Style

Recipes for rooms that are comfortable, pleasing, and timeless

ROS BYAM SHAW

RYLAND PETERS & SMALL
LONDON • NEW YORK

Senior designer Toni Kay
Senior commissioning editor
  Annabel Morgan
Production manager Gordana Simakovic
Art director Leslie Harrington
Editorial director Julia Charles
Publisher Cindy Richards

First published in 2021 by
Ryland Peters & Small
20–21 Jockey's Fields,
London WC1R 4BW
and
341 East 116th Street
New York, NY 10029

www.rylandpeters.com

10 9 8 7 6 5 4 3 2

ISBN 978-1-78879-242-4

A CIP record for this book is available
from the British Library.

Library of Congress CIP data has
been applied for.

Printed and bound in China

Contents

Introduction	6
The Hall	16
The Kitchen	36
Patina	66
The Utility Room	82
The Living Room	94
Antiques	120
The Bedroom	134
Fabrics	156
The Bathroom	170
Collections	186
Sources	200
Picture credits	203
Index	204
Acknowledgments	205
Perfect English Quotes	208

Introduction

Fourteen years ago, I was riding my bicycle along a Devon lane, bowling along between hedges fizzing with cow parsley, when I came up with an idea for a book. It would be called *Perfect English* – a gentle pun to introduce a selection of houses in a classic English vein; houses where dogs snoozed on squashy sofas, wisteria curled through sash windows, chintz curtains faded at the edges, plump roses in lustre jugs dropped petals on scrubbed kitchen tables, their scent mingling with the smell of beeswax furniture polish, old clocks ticked and chimed on the hour, floorboards creaked, and wood fires crackled.

The book was published in 2007, complete with an array of squashy sofas, roses, and chintz. Then came *Perfect English Cottage* and *Perfect English Farmhouse*, and in its small way, *Perfect English* had become a brand. Most recent in the series, published in 2018, was *Perfect English Townhouse*. And I am happy these books have worn well, mainly because the decoration of the houses featured in them has hardly dated. Despite suggestions – not all of them entirely serious – for *Perfect English Rectory*, *Perfect English Apartment*, and *Perfect English Bungalow*, it seemed time instead to take a broader look at the basic ingredients of this perennial style of decoration.

HISTORY

The interiors that I chose to feature in my books are variations on the style that has come to be known as English Country House. In its purest form, this is a way of furnishing and decorating that was crystallized, if not invented, in the middle of the last century by decorator John Fowler, and the wealthy American Nancy Lancaster, who bought Colefax & Fowler, the company that still bears Fowler's name. Nancy was a passionate and brilliant home-maker, who combined a love of the past, and an eye for scale, colour, and proportion, with American ideas of domestic comfort in three splendid 18th-century English

country houses she restored and lived in. Among many famous guests who enjoyed her hospitality, Cecil Beaton said of her house, Haseley, that it 'could not be more beautiful to the spirit', and praised her 'talent for … making a grand house appear less grand'.

Nancy understood how to introduce informality into rooms that might otherwise be intimidating. She did this partly by mixing furnishings of different styles, periods, and value, but also by 'knocking back' her interiors such that nothing looked too brash or showy, however high the ceilings or magnificent the chimney pieces. One of her many tricks was to dye new fabrics in a solution of tea in order to soften and age their colours. She was also known to leave loose/slip covers outside in sun and rain to weather them.

John Fowler had an equally peerless eye, and was encyclopaedic in his knowledge of historical interiors, particularly those of the 18th century. Between them, he and Nancy established a form of decoration that honoured the architecture of important houses, at the same time as making them lovely to live in. While Nancy's homes were stately, John Fowler's was a picturesque, miniature hunting lodge, the exquisite interiors of which proved their style equally applicable on a small scale. Above all, both wished to avoid pretension and to create rooms that looked mellow with age and use, even when freshly decorated and recently furnished.

PAGE 7 Antique prints and engravings hang in the entrance hall of an 18th-century townhouse. The long, narrow space is ideal for the display of detailed images such as these.

LEFT An original kitchen fireplace offers an alcove for a range cooker. The mantelshelf holds a mix of the decorative and the useful – stuffed birds, an ostrich egg, and a pot of wooden spoons.

BELOW LEFT The ancient oak frame of this medieval house, including a mullioned window in what was once an external wall, is on show in a bedroom.

OPPOSITE This is the image that was chosen for the first edition of *Perfect English*, and nicely makes the point that in order to be perfectly English, an interior needs to have imperfections.

PERFECT IMPERFECTION

A lack of perfection is the first, and perhaps the most fundamental, characteristic of this archetypal English look. As Roger Jones, Decorator and Head of Antiques at Sibyl Colefax & John Fowler, wryly commented, the book *Perfect English* should really have been called *Imperfect English*.

The title may have been a misnomer, but the point was made visually by the cover of the first edition. It shows a corner of the living room of antique dealers Matthew and Miranda Eden. A door stands ajar, its paint chipped where it has opened and closed year on year. To its right hangs a huge Victorian oil painting, canvas sagging a little and slightly torn, and in front of the painting sits a large and magnificently battered armchair, its feather seat cushion bulging through a ripped corner, its original floral upholstery patched with calico. Two big cushions covered in buttercup yellow silk damask slump across its seat and arms. I find it impossible to look at that chair without feeling a strong desire to sink into it. Irresistibly inviting and charmingly eccentric, it most certainly is not perfect.

The scruffiness exemplified by the Eden armchair, codified as 'shabby chic' and endlessly bowdlerized, belongs to a peculiarly English modesty that would rather minimize than exaggerate – for example, describing having a serious illness as being 'a bit under the weather' – and that shies away from ostentation when it comes to interiors, hence feeling the need to put a frayed Panama hat on an important marble bust. John Fowler called it 'humble elegance', and 'pleasing decay'. Nancy Lancaster aimed for 'a look of studied carelessness'.

MIXING IT UP

It was an Italian decorator, Renzo Mongiardino, who said that the secret of decorating was to 'mix the high with the low', for example using wicker chairs in a room hung with valuable works of art. This idea has been embraced by all of the greats, from Elsie de Wolfe and Madeleine Castaing to David Hicks. John Fowler and Nancy Lancaster were both past masters at shaking up the style cocktail – Fowler liked 'a dash of French', while Nancy insisted that every room should have in it 'something ugly', and famously likened the decorating of a room to making a salad.

This is how to make a room full of beautiful, rare, and covetable furnishings seem more approachable and down to earth. Most of us don't have to worry too much about an excess of valuable antiques creating a museum-like feel in our homes, but it's still worth remembering that a liquorice allsorts selection is always more interesting than wall-to-

wall 18th century or mid-century modern. If you can put them together – a Georgian mirror over a 1950s sideboard, say, with a modern vase and candlesticks spotted in a charity/thrift shop, finding echoes in their colours, lines, or proportions – you will create the surprise of unexpected contrasts. This is the decorating equivalent of an outfit that mixes vintage, designer, and high street. It requires a good eye, and a certain aesthetic courage. If you get it right, it should seem effortless.

COMFORT

Appearing to have tried too hard – anything that smacks of glossy hotel or show home – kills this look stone dead. A room must appear well-used and lived-in. Which brings us to another of its vital qualities – comfort. Heightened interior perfection – diehard minimalism, for example, or the state bedchambers of Versailles – can be soothing to

OPPOSITE A living room that exemplifies the relaxed feel created by a mix of furnishings of different dates and styles. The coffee table and swivel chair are both mid-century modern, but the two sofas are a traditional design.

RIGHT Antique and vintage textiles made up into cushions and an old patchwork quilt provide comfort and colour in a small cottage bedroom. The furnishings span the centuries and include an early 20th-century painted iron bed and a 1950s bedside lamp.

BELOW The kitchen of this 18th-century townhouse has been fitted with bespoke joinery with a period feel. Baskets are used as storage and the capacious sink is antique. Dry goods have been decanted into a set of matching storage jars that is displayed on the open shelving.

PAGES 12–13 This magnificent dresser fills one wall of a farmhouse kitchen. The base cupboards are antique, but the shelves above were specially made and each bracket is a silhouette portrait of a family member – a subtlety of design you only notice once it has been pointed out.

the eye, contemplative, ravishingly beautiful, but is not what most of us would call comfortable. It is hard to relax when your presence feels like an unattractive and untidy imposition. I love the look of an all-white interior, but I am always subliminally worried that I might spill coffee on the pristine sofa, or leave a grubby footprint on the snowy floor.

Domestic comfort requires harmony, balance, pleasing arrangements, pattern, and colour. It also means furnishings arranged to suit the way you like to live – supportive chairs around a steady table for dining, living-room sofas and armchairs placed to encourage conversation, with a side table for putting down a drink. Fabrics play a vital role, with curtains, cushions and rugs all contributing to that feeling of being cocooned and cradled. A generous use of fabrics ensures that acoustics, another component of comfort, are not harsh. Lighting is important – bright where needed, but otherwise soft enough to flatter a room and its occupants.

Practicality and convenience go hand in hand with comfort, although these are sometimes trumped in English interiors by aesthetics. Fitted carpets, for example, may be rejected in favour of rugs on bare boards, even though fitted carpet is good for draught-proofing, easy to vacuum, and won't trip you up. An Aga is arguably less user-friendly than an eye-level double oven, a roll-top bathtub can leave you with the problem of where to put the soap, and so on. On the other hand, it is very English – assuming the luxury of space – to have a boot room, a larder, a scullery, pantry or laundry room with extra sinks, and a capacious airing/hot cupboard complete with slatted wooden shelving.

NOSTALGIA

Which brings us to nostalgia. This is a way of decorating that foregrounds the past by favouring period architecture, and choosing antique and vintage furnishings over new. These are interiors where tradition is valued, where inherited pieces are kept for sentimental reasons, and decisions are prompted by childhood memories, whether that means cream gloss paint in a farmhouse kitchen, or glass used to panel the walls around a bathtub. Nostalgia also informs the preponderance of Agas, roll-top bathtubs, Belfast sinks, and rugs on bare floorboards.

GREEN

England is still green and pleasant, and English interiors make constant reference, whether with floral fabrics, jugs of daffodils, or geraniums on windowsills, to the English love of gardens, and the countryside. But this style is green in another, more significant respect, one that transcends aesthetics. Inadvertently, and without ever having jumped on a fashionable bandwagon, it offers a way of furnishing and decorating while minimizing waste and consumption. The wood used to fashion a piece of antique furniture was sawn from trees cut down long ago. It was more than likely worked by hand, requiring a minimum of fossil fuels and causing few, if any, emissions. By choosing to keep your

clothes in a Regency chest of drawers, eat your lunch from a Victorian pine table, or display and store your crockery on an old dresser, you are recycling as well as using and preserving something of lasting value.

If a style does not demand impeccable straight lines, immaculate surfaces, and faultless fabrics, there is space for things that have been mended and restored. The earth's resources don't need to be plundered if you are happy to use and live with things that are second-, third-, or fourth-hand. You can afford better quality if you are not buying new, and thereby avoid storing up shoddy furnishings that will inevitably end up as landfill. And because it is a style that is never exactly fashionable, nor does it become outmoded, meaning you don't have to keep updating.

The English look has its tropes. But it is not prescriptive. On the contrary, it is forgiving, favouring informality and a certain laissez-faire. It doesn't insist on everything matching, allowing you to mix things up, get things a bit wrong even, with freedom to encompass the personal – whether that is a collection of architectural prints or a bargain found at a flea market. And what is any appealing interior if not an expression of the way of life, the ideas, and creativity of the people who inhabit it?

Many of you may recognize rooms on the following pages from previous books published by Ryland Peters & Small, both by me and by other authors. Because this is a book that concentrates on elements of design, rather than the stories of owners and designers, I have limited the caption information to discussions of style. Owners, designers, and photographers are credited on page 203–4, and I am grateful to all of them for the talent and creativity that have made this book possible.

OPPOSITE The panelled walls of this early 18th-century London townhouse had been painted using modern paints. In order to recreate the patina that had been lost, the new paint was stripped back and replaced with a finish that has the mottled look of old distemper.

The Hall

A hall is an introduction. The exterior and front door have already given plenty of clues – the sort you pick up when you see someone you haven't met before across a room – but entering the hall is the beginning of a conversation. Will it be tidy, empty, plain? Will it be colourful and crowded? As the first space you experience, it creates a lasting impression, ideally one of welcome. But a hall has an equally important practical role, as the stepping stone between indoors and outdoors, the passage between rooms, and, more often than not, the link between downstairs and upstairs.

The demands of practicality depend on the architecture and layout. If you live in a flat, then visitors may have passed through a communal hall, wiping their feet and shaking off their umbrellas before they get to your door. A detached house, especially one in the country, is likely to have a back door that is used more frequently than the front one, depending on where you park your car. This entrance may have its own hall where you can pull off muddy boots and wet coats, leaving the main entrance hall free to impress guests. Most terraced townhouses, on the other hand, are entered from the pavement, so these are hallways that have to work hard – though mud is less likely to be a problem.

In small houses, the hall has often become a casualty in the drive to optimize space. Where a front door opens directly into a narrow passage with the stairs ahead and rooms to one side, the temptation is to knock down these dividing walls, creating a single, larger room. This has an opening-up effect, bringing light to what might otherwise have been a dark staircase. On the other hand, you lose that useful intermediate area, however small, and the option of shutting doors in order to keep warmth and noise contained. You also sacrifice wall space, for coat hooks and shoe racks, and in the living room for placing furniture and hanging pictures. Most of all, you lose the moment of introduction that leaves you anticipating what is to come.

Even in houses with back doors and boot rooms, a hall is a well-worn path, and because of this its flooring should be hard-wearing. This is not a place for thick-pile carpet, valuable rugs, or anything that stains or weathers unattractively. Any of the traditional floorings used in period homes fit the bill. Floorboards, farmhouse flags or tessellated encaustic tiles – all look better for the polish endowed by generations of boot soles. This wear is difficult to fake. If you are not fortunate enough to have original flooring – and it is sad how often this is the case in old houses – a good alternative is to hunt down reclaimed versions, whether wood, stone, or ceramic. If this is too expensive or difficult to find, choose a material that suits the character and vernacular of the house and that might once have been used in it – a native wood, or local stone, brick, or terracotta tiling. The marble flooring of a stately home may have been imported from Italy, but most housebuilders of the past would have used something more readily available. Rugs and runners look good on hard flooring, and help to deaden the clatter of feet, but should also be hard-wearing and laid on top of non-slip underlay.

As for furnishings, this depends on the size of a hall, and whether it is the only place to hang coats, prop umbrellas, and line up footwear. I like the look of a row of coat hooks in a hall, and even a line of shoes, though you may want to

PAGE 16 The unusual design of the banister rail in this Regency townhouse is all the more striking for the lack of carpet on the stone stairs. Floorboards are also bare. Pattern is provided by a bold, geometric wallpaper, which suits the robust, generously scaled architecture of the house.

OPPOSITE Plain, stylish, and proof that the narrow hall typical of 18th and early 19th-century townhouses need not be dull. Chequerboard ceramic tiling, laid on the diagonal and framed by a border of plain tiles, is both handsome and practical.

PAGES 20–21 A large hall is useful, if communal, extra space. In this stone-built cottage it is home to the family piano – an arrangement that encourages a quick tune in passing.

put these in baskets or on racks for ease of cleaning the floor underneath. In a long, narrow hall, it is better to keep furnishings to one side, whether a bench or a console table, or a pair of hall chairs, all useful for dumping keys and bags. This is the place for a grandfather clock, standing flat against the wall, its rhythmic tick-tock a comforting heartbeat, its chime on the hour audible from other rooms.

Furnishings may be limited by space, but you can cover the walls with pictures, and carry on up the stairs. The best sort for smaller halls are those that benefit from scrutiny, as in a tight space you won't be looking at them from a distance. Architectural prints, cartoons with captions, fine drawings, small watercolours, maps – all can be enjoyed at close quarters. Mirrors also work well for a quick squint to see if your hat is straight and also, if strategically placed opposite a door, for example, to offer reflections that give the illusion of extra space, and bounce back borrowed light.

In a big hall you can go to town with furnishings, whether a grand piano – though it will be heard throughout the house if you decide to sit down and play – or a table piled with books, and centred by a big vase of flowers. Sometimes a larger hall can be appropriated as an occasional dining room. The table piled with books can become the dining table, and chairs can be imported from elsewhere. There is something fine about dining in a hall. Gathering at the centre of a house, as in a medieval great hall, confers a sense of occasion – added to which is the novelty that comes with transforming a space for different use. Most dedicated dining rooms are infrequently used and have the slightly forlorn, stale feel of being 'saved for best'. Which is why I have not devoted a chapter to them.

OPPOSITE Old floorboards, polished by generations of passing feet, make ideal flooring for a hall – both hard-wearing and beautiful. In this early 18th-century house, the original staircase with its elegant, turned banisters also survives and has been left unpainted.

ABOVE The hall of this early 19th-century London mansion flat had no particular architectural merit, but has been given great panache by the use of a large-scale wallpaper by Farrow & Ball above a dado/chair rail. The arrangement of engravings over a needlework chair with an equally big pattern placed opposite the front door creates an immediate visual impact.

RIGHT The narrow winding staircase typical of a terraced townhouse offers a large expanse of wall that's ideal for a tessellation of pictures, particularly those that benefit from close inspection such as fine drawings and engravings.

ABOVE No family needs quite as many coat hooks, nor as many wellington boots, but this inner hall in a country house hotel could be replicated on a small scale with its smart benches, storage baskets, and high shelving.

OPPOSITE The expanse of wall next to a staircase is often the biggest empty wall space in a house, and can either be filled with pictures or with lavish pattern; here, the big, painterly flowers and birds of 'Adam's Eden' wallpaper from Lewis & Wood.

ABOVE LEFT A cottage landing – effectively an upstairs hall – has old floorboards painted in a zebra stripe, while the wooden stairs that lead up to attic bedrooms have been left as they were found when the carpet was stripped off, in a patchwork of old paint colours. Paint is an inexpensive way to decorate a wooden floor, and a good way to disguise stained and damaged boards.

ABOVE RIGHT This Regency staircase has wooden treads treated with a dark stain to complement the collection of horned trophies that cover the wall of the half landing. The wooden donkey adds a further sculptural element.

LEFT Another plain hall in an 18th-century house, furnished with a simple wooden bench. Shoes are lined up so neatly that they have become a decorative element in this otherwise sparsely furnished space.

OPPOSITE Stairs at the far end of the entrance hall of a London townhouse lead down to the lower ground floor. The angle in the wall has been furnished with an array of coat hooks, tucked tidily away here where they cannot be seen from the front door.

PAGE 28 The gracious sweep of stairs in a country house hallway is highlighted by a pillar box red carpet. In a hall that is otherwise furnished traditionally, with a grandfather clock, and gilt-framed oil paintings, this cascade of bold colour adds glamour.

PAGE 29 A hall with no window and cottage proportions might not seem an obvious candidate for a dark colour. In fact, the rich purple of the walls ensures a theatrical entrance and contrasts with the brightness of the rooms leading off it.

LEFT In a large country house, where there is space for boots and coats to be kept elsewhere, a hall can be furnished for looks above practicality, such as this arrangement of antique furnishings, lamp, mirror, and objects that are purely decorative.

BELOW Hung traditionally on chains from a picture rail, this staircase hall is a gallery of architectural engravings that can be enjoyed on the way up and down stairs, or from the vantage point of the galleried landing.

RIGHT Keeping the decoration plain and simple in a hall serves to emphasize its architectural features; in this house, a beautifully turned wooden newel post, arched opening, and panelled doors. A coir mat with bound edges is matched by the same matting used up the stairs.

OPPOSITE A big hallway demands furnishings to match; here, large oil paintings and substantial table lamps, which flank an architectural model of the house. Baskets of kindling stand ready for use in the fireplaces of reception rooms on either side of the hall.

ABOVE LEFT The original fielded panelling and charmingly crooked staircase of this early 18th-century townhouse need little in the way of additional decoration. The rich red of the runner creates a warm sense of welcome.

ABOVE RIGHT To have a hall that is large enough to accommodate a piano is without a doubt a spatial luxury. This hall is big enough for a baby grand, which fits neatly beneath the slope of the cantilevered stairs. Treads and banisters are painted white, throwing them into relief against the darker walls.

LEFT Another landing, and one that illustrates the importance of views through into other rooms from hallways. This particular example is made harmonious by a green stair carpet, its colour echoed in the rooms beyond.

OPPOSITE This rustic hallway, with its primitive ladder staircase, is enlivened by warm, bright colour. The piano under the stairs has quite a different feel to the grandeur of the same arrangement in the hallway shown above right. The staircase wall is lined with shallow bookshelves, in a clever use of limited space.

The Kitchen

Kitchens have been on the up for a good hundred years. No longer hidden from polite society in dank basements or distant wings, the kitchen has come to be the room on which typically most expense is lavished. Cooking is on show, and the kitchen table is where family and friends gather to eat and socialize, and, when not laid for a meal, is also likely to be where laptops congregate, homework is done, board games are played, flowers are arranged, and plans are made. Once a Cinderella, kept in the background and never introduced to guests, the 21st-century kitchen has stepped into the limelight.

This relatively new status often causes a problem in old houses where the rooms with the best light, views, proportions, and architectural detailing were always designed to be reception rooms, never kitchens. Some townhouse basement kitchens have decent ceiling heights and, with a bit of excavating outside at the back, can be persuaded to open directly into the garden instead of the original window well below ground level. An alternative is to elevate the kitchen to the raised ground floor reception rooms. But this can leave you short of a living room, and wondering how best to use a dark basement. In country houses, the kitchen is invariably on the ground floor, but may be north-facing and have the least attractive aspect. Again, the solution can be to relocate to a former reception room, if planning regulations allow. Farmhouses, where the kitchen has always played an important role at the centre of family life, are an exception, and the term 'farmhouse kitchen' is bandied about by estate agents as a mark of the highest approbation.

Fitted kitchens were still a novelty in the mid-20th century, an American import, seen as a little flashy, if appealing for their perceived efficiency and hygiene. They soon became the norm, and by the 1960s, Formica in a variety of cheerful colours was widely used to create wall-to-wall wipe-clean surfaces. In the 1980s, when English Country House style had an ebullient renaissance, the fitted kitchen was adapted to suit, decked out in dragged paintwork, with multi-pane glazed wall cupboards like rows of dinky cottage windows, and shaped corner shelves edged with ranks of miniature turned spindles. Recently, a more grown-up and sophisticated style of fitted kitchen, based on the utilitarian and slightly ascetic pantries, sculleries, dairies, and larders of large country houses, has become the kitchen of choice for a period home.

A fitted kitchen made in solid wood, with recessed hinges and drawers with dovetail joints, is a fine thing, but requires a substantial budget. Fortunately for the fan of English style, an unfitted kitchen, or one that is a mix of fitted and unfitted pieces, is just as desirable. This ideally requires a reception room-sized space. That classic kitchen trio of Aga (or range cooker), dresser, and a sturdy and generously proportioned kitchen table takes up a lot of space. Space also allows for pictures on the wall, and for pieces of antique and vintage furniture – sideboards, cabinets, plate racks, and wall shelves – that contribute to the decorative interest. A dresser may be used for display as well as for storage – the ideal showcase for a motley selection of old blue and white china. If there is a place for a couple of armchairs, all the better. This emphasis on comfort, and the inclusion of things that are beautiful as well as practical, is typically English.

It might be as well at this point to explore the English obsession with that large, hugely heavy, solid metal stove, the Aga. It was invented in 1922 by a Swedish physicist determined to improve on his wife's old-fashioned kitchen range with something cleaner, less dangerous, and permanently hot and ready for use. Seven years later, a British company bought the licence, and Agas have been made and coveted here ever since, achieving totemic status as the epitome of domestic comfort. The permanent source of heat is cosy in our damp climate. My children used to sit on our Aga, bottoms insulated by the oven cloth, to warm up in our cold old house. Aga lovers are devoted, not only to the way the ovens cook with minimal loss of moisture, but to their general usefulness. The tops of their lids are hot enough to dry laundry, and the perfect place to rejuvenate soggy socks and damp newspapers. You can make toast directly on the hot plates. In four-oven versions, the warming oven is just the right temperature to revive a chilly, orphan lamb, or any other small, bedraggled animal. The longer you live with an Aga – I inherited one 20 years ago as an Aga sceptic – the more ways you find to use them – to desiccate rose petals for potpourri, for example, or to melt drips of wax off candlesticks. Modern Agas are adjustable and can run on electricity and, of course, there are other makes of this type of range cooker.

Agas and armchairs are not an option for many kitchens, and where space is limited, a fitted kitchen makes by far the best use of it. Even a small fitted kitchen can be given a relaxed, English feel with the addition of a few pieces that don't match – an old plate rack on the wall, or a ladderback chair, always useful for hanging a tea towel or sitting on in a break from stirring and chopping. You might also consider having curtains instead of doors on lower cupboards – a cheap and pretty option. Any washable fabric is suitable, gathered and hung on curtain hooks, or threaded onto a pole or curtain wire. Ginghams and stripes have a simple, rustic feel, but you can be more adventurous with scale and colour to good effect. Photographer Jan Baldwin has curtains in a wide red and white diagonal in her London kitchen, which look strikingly chic (see page 50). Open shelves, to display china or earthenware, or old enamel storage jars, and a rail for hanging utensils such as sieves, colanders, and ladles all add to the mismatched effect.

In the final count, efficiency is not the priority in this style of English kitchen. If a catering kitchen with ceramic tiling, strip lighting, and expanses of gleaming stainless steel is at one end of the spectrum, these kitchens are at the opposite end, where choices such as flooring, lighting, and work surfaces may be dictated more by aesthetics than by ease of cleaning, and durability. Wood, stone, brick, and terracotta all have the right, traditional feel. And pendant lights, whether with enamel, china, or metal shades, look better than recessed spotlights.

PAGE 36 Cream gloss paint on walls and ceilings is a traditional wipe-clean choice in a farmhouse kitchen, with a vintage cream Aga to match. The original fitted cupboards are raised above floor level in case of mice.

OPPOSITE The jolly blue and white stripes of Cornish pottery ranged on narrow shelves make a decorative focus in a small kitchen, as well as providing useful and conveniently placed storage.

The problem of placing a
modern kitchen in rooms
that would once have been
reception rooms in an early
19th-century house has
here been elegantly solved
with an Aga in an enlarged
fireplace embrasure, a sleek
contemporary kitchen island,
and a wall of traditionally
panelled fitted cupboards
and drawers.

ABOVE An Aga stove has the reassuring solidity of the old-fashioned kitchen range it was designed to supersede, while blue distemper harks back to a time when the colour was thought to deter flies.

OPPOSITE The rustic feel of this country kitchen is emphasized by the texture of the rough stonework that has been painted but not plastered, and the collection of baskets hanging from the ceiling beams.

OPPOSITE In a completely unfitted cottage kitchen, an old butcher's block makes as solid a work surface as you could wish for. The wittily makeshift stick suspended on string from a ceiling beam and hung with utensils is like an arty kitchen-themed mobile.

ABOVE AND ABOVE RIGHT Brick is the unifying theme of another unfitted country kitchen, tiling the floor, supporting the old stoneware sink, and painted with limewash on the walls. A custom-made table with a zinc top serves as a long work surface with open shelves beneath for storage. The planked wall behind the refrigerator was kept as found, but moved forward a couple of feet to make space for a larder behind it.

RIGHT The textures of old brick flooring, a wooden work surface, and the ancient wooden framework of what was originally an outer wall complete with window are all highlighted in this lean-to kitchen by snowy expanses of plain white paintwork.

LEFT Everything in this country kitchen announces a rural lifestyle, from the informal bunches of garden flowers and the stoneware pots of jam with their gingham mob caps to the simplicity of the unlined curtain threaded onto curtain wire. White walls and a concrete floor painted pale grey are the blank canvas for these splashes of bright colour.

OPPOSITE In an unfitted kitchen that defies convention, a set of Victorian shelves on casters holds cutlery/flatware, china, and glasses, but also a horse's skull and a knitted cauliflower under a glass dome. Meanwhile, hanging from hooks beneath the shelf are pebbles, feathers, and photographs tied up with ribbon – a mix of the useful and utilitarian with the decorative and whimsical.

PAGES 48–49 A townhouse kitchen that is part-fitted, part-unfitted and furnished with pieces that are antique, vintage, and contemporary. Plaster above picture-rail level has been left complete with its mottled history after stripping, and a redundant doorway has been converted to make a 'coffee corner'.

OPPOSITE AND ABOVE An example of a lower ground floor kitchen in a London townhouse where the floor has been dug down to give extra ceiling height, the original two rooms have been knocked into one, and the garden excavated to make it on a level with French doors at the back. The result is a spacious room that is also an object lesson in how to create a memorable effect with simple ingredients, notably the strong diagonal stripe of the Neisha Crosland curtaining.

OPPOSITE In line with the architecture of a room designed to be a reception room, the chairs and table in this townhouse kitchen are particularly elegant examples of country antiques, and the island is panelled to match the original panelled doors.

ABOVE Wallpaper remains unusual in a kitchen, but in an age when a big kitchen is used for entertaining and as a family living room as much as somewhere to cook and eat, it is ever more appropriate.

RIGHT It can be difficult to find
enough suitable pieces of old and
reclaimed furniture to create a
wholly unfitted kitchen with sufficient
drawers, cupboards, and practical
work surfaces. Supplementing
antiques such as this glass-fronted
wall cabinet with some areas of
fitted cabinetry is the best of both
worlds, creating a look that is
informal and relaxed.

PAGES 56–57 In a kitchen this size, it is possible to have it all – plentiful storage, a table big enough for family and friends, plus a comfortable armchair. The symmetrical arrangement of the cupboards and the central placing of the large island unit are happily in tune with the architecture of a classically proportioned 18th-century country house.

OPPOSITE A lesson in how to give character and distinction to a galley kitchen in an urban flat using unusual colours – a floor in gloss lilac, khaki walls, and a primrose yellow blind – plus decorative elements such as the framed pictures, and open shelves holding books, pretty china, and bright orange enamelled cooking pots.

BELOW This large room in a period house has been 'zoned', with a cooking area created by placing an electric Aga centrally and building a three-quarter-height wall behind it – a clever way to separate cooking and dining areas.

PAGE 60 A new fitted kitchen in the basement of a late 18th-century townhouse that, thanks to its painted panelled doors, cornicing/crown molding above the cabinet, and traditional knobs and handles, looks as though it might always have been there.

PAGE 61 This new extension to an old cottage has a pitched roof, giving the kitchen a feel of spaciousness beyond its footprint. A floor of reclaimed terracotta tiles helps the flow between the original and the modern parts of the house.

LEFT A low-key fitted kitchen in a design simple enough to be timeless occupies one end of a large room, originally the drawing room in a house that dates back to the 15th century. The 19th-century floorboards are sanded rather than polished, in keeping with the new informality.

OPPOSITE This cottage kitchen is a later extension, hence its generous size and the thickness of the wall between it and the room next to it. The old outer wall has been painted but not replastered to give a rustic effect that's only intensified by the quarry tiles, a plate rack, and a rusty garden table.

OPPOSITE A larder has been created at one end of this cottage kitchen by walling off a corner under the sloping roof, affording hidden storage space for less visually appealing kitchen essentials – but evidently no space for cookery books.

ABOVE A small kitchen in what was once the scullery of an early 18th-century house has been brought alive by rich colour. A set of open shelves offers easily accessible storage, plus an opportunity for display.

Patina

There are many ways to ruin the atmosphere and period feel of an old house. You can strip out the original windows and replace them with double-glazed uPVC replicas. You can prise up floorboards and stick down new ones without holes, gaps, or inconvenient slopes. Uneven flags can be replaced with smooth limestone that lies perfectly straight and flat. And if you want to be thorough, you can hack off old lime plaster with its waves and wobbles and soft corners, and replaster with gypsum, being sure to get sharp right angles by using metal corner strips. If you do any or all of these things, you will have lost something irreplaceable. Patina, as well as the craftsmanship of the past, is what you throw away.

Patina describes the alterations to the surface of a material that occur over time through exposure to the elements, or through use. As a term of approval, it is applied to materials that are robust enough to last and continue to look beautiful – usually natural materials such as stone, wood, and leather. A plastic garden chair will acquire a different finish if left outside for long enough, but the effect would probably not be described as patina. Old buildings acquire patina, both inside and out, and being careful to preserve it is the difference between sensitive restoration and over-restoration.

In the antiques trade, the patina of a piece of furniture is a key element of its desirability and value. If it is wood, it will have acquired a depth of colour and sheen conferred by generations of dusters and polish. A painted piece dating from the 18th or 19th century may have been worn bare around its handles, its colours may have faded, its pattern become faint, but it will have achieved the 'pleasing decay' so loved by decorator John Fowler. Old mirror glass, backed with mercury, develops a mottling of grey, blurring the edges of reflections with a romantic silvery dust. The raised edges of gilding rub away to reveal its dark red ground or the white of the silky gesso beneath. Antique fabrics fade according to the resilience of the vegetable dyes used to colour them. It is only by looking at the back of a 17th-century tapestry

where the threads have been protected from sunlight that you see how its subdued, subtle palette of blues and browns was once vibrant with green, yellow, red, and purple.

Patina is a slow process, though there are ways of hurrying it up for effect. Unscrupulous antique dealers have been known to attack a piece of furniture with a bicycle chain in an attempt to mimic the ravages of time, and there was recently a fashion for self-consciously chipped painted furnishings, labelled as 'shabby chic'. Some methods of ageing have better results than others. As already mentioned, Nancy Lancaster resorted to soaking new fabrics in a solution of tea, or leaving them outside in the rain for a few days to soften up and to take the edge off their colours and patterns.

English Country House style relies on patina for its charm, or even its essence. This is the source of that elusive and alluring sense of timeless comfort – the feeling that a room and its contents have been used and enjoyed, treasured and cared for. Chips and knocks, places where a stone floor has been eroded by endless steps, handles rubbed smooth by fingers and palms, fabrics bleached by the sun, all give us permission to add our own pennyworth of wear and tear. Patina is more than skin deep. In its unobtrusive way, it reminds us of our own mortality – of those who went before, and those who will come after us. This is why it is precious.

PAGE 67 Imagine how different this bedroom would look – how much atmosphere and character it would have lost – if there were fitted carpet and a fresh coat of vinyl emulsion. Instead, the time-worn elm floorboards are bare, and later layers have been scraped back to reveal original paint, faded and mottled, but intensely evocative and romantic.

LEFT Now a kitchen, this room was originally the dairy of this 18th-century farmhouse, and retains its limewashed walls, and slate floor polished to a gentle shine by centuries of feet. The old slate shelving has been reused as work surfaces.

BELOW LEFT Another kitchen with its original slate flags. In old houses, stone flags are often laid directly onto compressed earth, so it is best not to seal them, which traps damp and causes the stone to decay. The sheen of constant wear is better looking and better for the floor.

OPPOSITE A living room in which almost everything is patinated, from the wallpaper to the picture frames. And if patina could correctly be used to describe fabrics, it would equally apply to the rug with its rubbed pile, and the lengths of faded cotton toile draped over the sofa.

PAGE 70 A mural by master of painted decoration Adam Calkin, cleverly aged to look as though it might pre-date the stained and slightly tattered Victorian tailor's dummy that stands in front of it.

PAGE 71 ABOVE LEFT Natural materials tend to age well, often becoming more beautiful over time, like the leather of this antique sofa, worn to the deep gloss of a fresh conker.

PAGE 71 ABOVE RIGHT The painted stripes are not as old as the strips of wood used to panel this room, but wear and tear has not been overpainted, so the effect is one of seamless ageing.

PAGE 71 BELOW LEFT Leaving an old lime plaster wall unpainted after stripping off later paint and paper invariably results in a surface of intriguing colour and texture, like an ancient map.

PAGE 71 BELOW RIGHT Old mirror glass tends to decay in patches of silver speckling where the mercury compound used to back it has started to oxidize, resulting in mistily flattering reflections.

ABOVE Contrasts are decorating catnip, whether in terms of scale, colour, or texture. In this farmhouse kitchen, with its cracked stone flooring, flaking limewash, and bleached ceiling planks, the pair of contemporary plywood chairs look all the more pristine for their well-weathered setting.

OPPOSITE The same effect is achieved in this urban apartment, where a new kitchen and fresh white paint are set against original and well-scuffed floorboards, and a border of stripped plaster above the picture rail.

ABOVE LEFT Another example of lime plaster that has been stripped but not repainted. One of the appeals of this is how different the results can be – here, a subtle effect that's almost like stone.

ABOVE Blue limewash paint used on the brick wall in a corner of a big country house kitchen, and already dappled like a summer sky veiled in wispy cloud.

LEFT Distemper and limewash are types of paint that tend to fade and weather, and are a good option if you want a wall surface that does not look too uniform or spanking new. This blue limewash makes a soft background for a cupboard, the brown paint of which has started gently to decay.

OPPOSITE The walls of this drawing room in the late 16th-century tower of an earlier house are freshly coated in white limewash, and it is the furnishings and fabrics that show their age, including a large cushion in antique velvet, much of its pile having worn away.

OPPOSITE Panelling and 'drab' paintwork survived in this East London townhouse, much of it under later layers, partly due to the poverty that afflicted the area through the 19th and 20th centuries. Carefully preserved in all its shabby glory, the interior retains a pungent sense of history.

ABOVE LEFT Original floorboards in an old house are rare and to be treasured. On this upstairs landing, the boards have been left unpolished, just as they might have been when the house was first built.

ABOVE RIGHT The owners of this 18th-century country house were fortunate to find an original paint scheme of bands of colour when they stripped off the later paper and paint from the walls of their hall.

RIGHT Decorators Rivière Interiors have used their own recipe of paint, which includes chalk dust, for the 18th-century panelling of this drawing room in order to replicate the effect of old distemper.

PAGES 78–79 Who knows when limewash was last applied to the walls and woodwork of this cottage bathroom? Again, it is the contrast with the unblemished white enamel and china of the bathtub and basin that makes this tiny room so visually interesting (not to mention the shark pinioned behind a beam).

OPPOSITE Wooden panelling, painstakingly dry scraped back to a colour scheme of pale grey dating from the second half of the 17th century. The glass of the mirror is similarly distressed, and the gilding of the antique chair has also been softened by time and use.

RIGHT A vintage pink washbasin looks particularly rosy and resplendent in a bathroom where the walls have been stripped and left bare.

BELOW The original floorboards in the bedroom of a farmhouse that dates to the Middle Ages slope so violently that two legs of the bed are propped on wooden blocks to keep it reasonably level. At some stage in the past, gaps between the boards were mended with strips of tin.

The Utility Room

A big Victorian country house had multiple utility rooms: a scullery adjacent to the kitchen for washing up and cleaning vegetables, a butler's pantry where tableware was kept, larders for storing food, and a laundry. There may also have been a gun room, a boot room, a dairy where butter and cheese were made, a stillroom for concocting cordials, jellies and jams, and a bakehouse.

Needless to say, these rooms were the domain of the serving staff employed to keep a large household running like clockwork, and to ensure that owners and guests enjoyed undisturbed comfort. Today's equivalent is a grand hotel. At home, most of us make do with a kitchen and its appliances – a dishwasher, washing machine, and a range of other electric gadgets that have taken the place of elbow grease.

To have a utility room of any description is a luxury. The same applies to a larder, a boot room, or a capacious airing/hot cupboard. If you are fortunate enough to have space to spare beyond the cupboard under the stairs, these are places where the satisfactions of good housekeeping can be indulged.

Many old houses still have larders – small rooms with small windows that may have metal mesh instead of glass for maximum ventilation, and slate shelving that helped to keep things cool in an age before refrigeration. An airy larder is still a better place than a refrigerator to keep cheese, potatoes, onions, and fruit that you don't want to ripen too quickly. And filling the shelves can be a pleasure. If you make jam or chutney, you can line it up, complete with handwritten labels, and gingham caps tied with twine. You can decant dry goods into jars, store cakes in vintage tins, and string up home-grown garlic, onions, and bunches of dried herbs from the garden. Add a collection of vases and jugs for flowers, and this will fast become your favourite room – not just because of its utility, or because of the sense of security that comes with the modest stockpiling it allows, but because it will be so visually pleasing.

I have particularly strong memories of cupboards and back rooms in houses I have written about over the years: a walk-in china cupboard, stacked floor to ceiling with dinner and tea services, the boot room of a keen rider where boots stood in polished ranks, a laundry room where the owner had gone to the trouble of decanting the washing and cleaning liquids into a beautiful array of carefully labelled old glass bottles. Most enviable of all was an airing/hot cupboard with long shelves, each piled with neatly folded sheets, blankets, pillowcases, tablecloths, and napkins, all tied into sets with red ribbon, and a parcel label attached. It looked charming, and how marvellous never to pull out a sheet and find you have a single instead of the double you were looking for. This is an idea you can copy on a small scale, though you need discipline to keep it up.

These are aspirations. But there is much to be said for making the hard-working areas of a house as attractive, as well as practical, as possible. This is the place for a deep Belfast sink, ideal for washing vegetables and conditioning flowers. A wooden draining board looks right, and is a pleasure to use. Open shelving can be supported on handsome metal or shaped wooden brackets, and lower shelving can be prettily curtained. And in the same way that you can go to town with colour and pattern in a downstairs cloakroom because it is small and only visited briefly, utility rooms are somewhere you can be as eccentric as you like, whether hanging a picture you love that doesn't fit anywhere else, or lining up your flock of china swans.

Deliver Veg 4·30
Meet train 4·45

PAGE 83 A lovely combination of the old-fashioned and timeless – onions hanging from a nail, a wooden laundry rack on a pulley, a capacious stone sink, flagged floors, and a big zinc tub – with the power of modern plumbing.

OPPOSITE This large laundry room, with its row of washing and drying machines and ample ceiling height for clothes airers, services a big country house. Plenty of drawers and cupboards leave open shelves free for the visually pleasing.

RIGHT The oldest part of an old farmhouse, still with its medieval wooden mullions. Later this room became the dairy, and it is now the perfect place to store wine with its cool brick floor and small window.

BELOW RIGHT An abundance of hooks, shelves, and a plate rack in a scullery that also has the benefit of a modern dishwasher.

PAGE 86 Modern joinery mimicking antique, complete with ventilated cupboard doors for storing cheese and other foodstuffs, in the newly created larder of a large country house.

PAGE 87 This pantry in a German house with a very English feel retains all its original early 20th-century cupboards and drawers, which wrap round the room and extend from floor to ceiling – just as useful as when they were first installed.

OPPOSITE If you live in the country, a boot room can seem more necessity than indulgence – a mud-proof space for hanging damp coats, leaving dirty boots, storing logs, and keeping baskets that are useful for all kinds of things, from bringing in vegetables to collecting flower heads when deadheading.

ABOVE With its mustard paintwork, huge slate sink, and pebble work on the wall, this is an inspiring example of how to make a boiler and utility room beautiful. The rustic fruit-picking ladder, which looks as though it might just bend over and walk out through the door, has been put to use for hanging garlic.

RIGHT Shelves and hooks loaded with glass and crockery in the corner of a larder.

PAGE 90 Glorious buttercup yellow tiling in a sunny larder that has retained its original slate top on whitewashed brick piers as well as wooden shelving on decorative metal brackets.

PAGE 91 A big hall with a stone floor can double as a boot room when there is space for a long line of coat hooks. Wooden shelving beneath holds shoes stacked on top, and boots ranked beneath. The wooden gate stops dogs, and toddlers, from climbing the stairs.

ABOVE These two adjoining utility rooms in a country house have space for everything from hand-dipped beeswax candles, which drape over coat hooks, to items of crockery that neatly slot into the openings of old sets of drawers mounted above the deep stoneware sink.

OPPOSITE A painted bas-relief of a near life-sized bull oversees proceedings in the laundry room of a London flat; an invaluable working space made pretty with the thickly ruffled gathers of its stripy curtaining.

The Living Room

I have said this is not a prescriptive style, and in most respects it isn't. However, there are certain elements of the English living room – or drawing room, if you prefer the more old-fashioned term – that are non-negotiable. There should be a sofa, ideally squashy, plump, and larded with cushions – the sort of sofa you can curl up in, lie down on, and share with your dog. Armchairs can be substituted for the sofa, if necessary, as long as they are the sort you can sprawl in. The room needs a focus, a direction in which to point the sofa, and this can only be a fireplace. Best of all is an open fire, piled with logs snapping with flames in winter, its grate cool and dark on summer evenings when doors stand ajar into the garden.

Sofa and fireplace are the axis around which all other elements of the room are built. For comfort and convenience, these should include side tables big enough to hold a drink, a book, and a lamp, and perhaps a padded stool between sofa and fireplace for more books and somewhere to put a tea tray. Once you have these, you have everything you need. The same formula applies whether your room is large and high-ceilinged with tall sash windows and an ornate cornice, or cosy and beamed with a broad inglenook fireplace. All that changes is the number and positioning of sofas and armchairs, the intention being to create a conversational group in front of those dancing flames.

When it comes to filling the gaps, this is a room where style and creativity are on show. It is the most public room in the house, but unlike the kitchen, which you may also use for entertaining, it has a less specific role. Its purpose is mainly for rest and relaxation, and as a place to gather and talk. So once seating and lighting are sorted, with sofas, armchairs, and table lamps, it is the place to display any furnishing trophies – the inherited secretaire, the oil painting you splashed out on, the expensive rug. Ideally, these are pieces you have gathered over time, things you have been given, or have bought because they delight you, things that confer a little jolt of pleasure whenever you look at them.

No one can tell you what these things should be – there is no magic formula – but, as discussed in the introduction, it is the mix of furnishings, including pictures on the walls, curtains, upholstery fabrics, rugs, and ornaments, that give a room its character and atmosphere. This can mean not only pieces from different eras, but also different cultures – a Turkish suzani thrown over the back of a sofa, a group of Indian miniatures on the wall, an African basket.

In truth, this mix is difficult to get just right. The best decorators make it look easy. A master like Robert Kime can put an 18th-century painted Italian cupboard, a French provincial table, an English wing chair, curtains made from Anatolian tent hangings, a Turkish rug, and a 1920s standard lamp all in the same room, and create an effect that is harmonious, and looks very like the result of years of thoughtful acquisition by several generations of owners. This 'layering' is at the heart of what makes an English room distinctive. Because it is inclusive, it makes you feel welcome, and because there appear to be no strict rules, you feel you can relax.

For those of us who are not professional decorators with long experience and generous budgets, getting it right is likely to be a process of experiment – adding and subtracting, moving things round until you get what Nancy Lancaster

called 'a judicious mixture that flows'. Scale is also important – oddly, big bits of furniture look marvellous in small rooms, while lots of small pieces look as mincing and bitty in small rooms as they do in big ones. Scale equally applies to textiles and wallpapers – a sprigged fabric to complement a bold tree of life, neat checks with blowsy chintz, stripes with paisley, plain on pattern and pattern on plain. To weave it all together, you need a palette of colours that brings out the best in each other instead of clashing and disagreeing. This is much more straightforward if you limit a room to shades of white and cream or taupe and coffee, but also too restrictive to be truly English. Better to find a colour thread or theme, perhaps taken from the curtains or the sofa upholstery, and work around it, remembering that you can't always predict what will please and what won't, so it's worth trying out different combinations.

Scale and harmony also apply to ornaments, their size and placing. Little things look better in herds than dotted around singly. Some, like pretty boxes, are best appreciated from above so could be laid out on a side table. Others are best seen in silhouette ranked along a mantelshelf. Just as you can play with patterns, colours, and scale, so you can twiddle the dials of symmetry in arrangements that subtly subvert expectations, setting up a framework with a pair of tall candlesticks, or matching jugs, and weaving things of differing heights and shapes in between. It's a game you can play endlessly to get different effects.

There is one last element that many would consider essential in a living room, and that is the television, assuming you do not have a secondary reception room, snug, or playroom where watching it can be indulged like a guilty secret. If the fireplace is the focal point of the room, then the television needs to be next to it. I have seen various ways of accommodating televisions – inside a cupboard, wall-mounted in a box behind doors from a glazed antique cabinet, and tucked under the heavily embroidered cloth of a corner table. As long as it is not so big that its blank, black oblong dominates, I would rather see it than not, though it is nice to be able to hide it on occasion, and I note that televisions have been censored in every photograph I have chosen to illustrate this chapter.

The cherry on the cake of a room made from these ingredients is fresh flowers – one of Nancy Lancaster's three 'tricks'. She suggested 'masses of them', along with open fires and candlelight. If you have a large and productive garden and time for flower arranging, or a generous flower budget, then you can follow Nancy's advice to the letter. If you live in the country, there are certain times of year when you can pick armfuls of cow parsley or foxgloves. For longer-lasting displays, there are pot plants, which are having a fashion moment. For something traditional, and typically English, you might choose pelargoniums, which some people can persuade to flower all year if kept indoors.

PAGE 95 A classic arrangement of a sofa facing the fire and attendant armchair. Plain pale colours on walls and upholstery are spiced up by the dusty yellow of the curtains and the rich reds and strong geometry of Turkish kilim rugs and cushions.

OPPOSITE Another room that contrasts plain walls in a neutral shade with warm colour, busy pattern, and a whole wall of close-hung pictures above the sofa.

PAGES 98–99 This grand, classical drawing room has so many ingredients that are typically English that it is hard to know where to begin. Perhaps most notable, along with the flowers and the casual cocktail of colour and pattern, is the presence of a magnificently relaxed and saggy sofa, layered with squishy cushions.

OPPOSITE The formality of this elegant panelled room, with its hang of antique portraits and selection of mostly 18th-century furnishings, is undercut and softened by enormous cushions on the demure French sofa and an untidy pile of books on the side table.

ABOVE When the arrangement of doors, windows, and fireplace allow, to have sofas facing each other on either side of a fireplace is comfortable and looks balanced. There is no need for them to match.

PAGE 102 In a small living room, there may hardly be space for a sofa, in which case a capacious armchair (or two) makes an excellent substitute.

PAGE 103 In a large drawing room, the basic elements of armchair, sofa, and coffee table or stool for books and the tea tray remain very similar but on a much bigger scale. This padded ottoman is expansive enough to provide extra seating alongside the tea tray; and what could be more English than afternoon tea in front of the fire?

LEFT English style at its most ascetic in the first-floor drawing room of an early 18th-century London townhouse. Although the floor is bare and the windows have shutters but no curtains, the English trope of sofas facing one another on either side of the fireplace persists.

PAGE 106 A traditional, elegant drawing room in an 18th-century house with space enough for large, draped side tables at one end of each sofa. Even in a smaller room, side tables are important for comfort, offering somewhere to put a lamp, a drink, a book, or the TV remote control.

PAGE 107 Tradition given a few glamorous tweaks with the upholstery and a cushion in leopard print, and an oval convex mirror hung over the overmantel mirror offering a condensed reflection of the whole room.

ABOVE Although sparsely furnished, this cottage living room is inviting thanks to the welcoming arms of the chair and its complement of cushions and knitted throw; an ideal place to sit in front of the fire with a good book.

LEFT Every chair, stool, and sofa in this Victorian recreation of a medieval great hall is upholstered in a different fabric. Add cushions and a rug and you have a wide range of colour and pattern in a mix that remains harmonious because of the way that red, blue, and mustard predominate.

OPPOSITE These armchairs are so plump and mounded with cushions, you feel you might bounce straight off them. Instead, thanks to squashy feather fillings, you can make a nest and then cover up in the woollen throws that hang over their backs.

A huge fireplace, heavy curtains, a big rug laid over matting, and velvet upholstery make this farmhouse living room particularly cosy, while the mix of furnishing styles and periods and the bright colours create a relaxed, bohemian look.

ABOVE If a living room is sufficiently large to offer more than one group of seating, a corner sofa is a comfortable and conversational way to provide it, here upholstered in a luscious strawberry red and with its own side and coffee tables.

OPPOSITE A series of disparate and sculptural pieces occupies the corner of this panelled drawing room, including a forged iron lamp, part of an old weather vane, and a venerable armchair with regal, lavishly scrolled wings.

RIGHT Rugs from Turkey and the Far East have long been a staple ingredient of English interiors. Here, the floor is plain and a kilim rug has been used to upholster the sofa.

BELOW LEFT In the drawing room of a grand country house, the placing of sofas, armchairs, and side tables remains the same, just on a larger scale and with ample space between them. The loose/slip covers create a more informal look than fitted upholstery.

BELOW RIGHT Faded antique fabrics and furnishings and an abundance of garden flowers in this archetypal English country living room.

PAGE 115 Lighting is hugely important. You may want bright lamps next to seating for reading by, but you cannot beat table lamps with cream shades placed in the corners of a living room for producing a gentle, atmospheric, and soothing ambience.

LEFT A constellation of tiny fairy lights and a scattering of pictures above the inglenook of a cottage living room make for a look that is playful and pretty.

BELOW Another cottage sitting room centred around a big open fire. Here, the various different fabrics are related, being mostly checks and stripes. This includes the rugs, one of them checked and the other striped, the checked one laid at an angle in order not to create a rigid grid.

OPPOSITE This gracious, panelled drawing room is almost too poised and chic to be typically English. The comfort of a deep sofa with a generous loading of cushions, a thick rug laid over the matting, and the deliberate disarray of books on the shelves help it to qualify, but still at the very smartest and tidiest end of the English-style spectrum.

ABOVE A balance of elegance and comfort in a large English country house drawing room, with sofas gathered around the fireplace, a padded stool piled with books, and a drinks tray at the ready.

OPPOSITE A chair by the fire, rush matting and a rug, warm pink walls, sunny yellow curtains, pens in a mug, books, and a reading light – what more could you wish for?

Antiques

There is not a room in this book, not a kitchen nor even a bathroom, that does not contain an antique: tables, beds, cabinets, chairs, sofas, kitchen dressers, chests of drawers, mirrors, paintings, prints, china, candlesticks, washbasins, boxes, light fittings, bedspreads, curtains, rugs, the list goes on. Antique furnishings are integral to this style of decorating, conveying a comfortable aura of continuity and tradition, and the impression that possessions have been slowly accrued, possibly by generations of the same family, even if in truth they were bought only yesterday.

Antiques add depth to a room, the charm of nostalgia, and the romance of imagining all those people from the past who knew and used them before you. Even as a child I preferred old things to new – my favourite doll had a bisque head and composition limbs with creaking joints, and my best toy was a ramshackle 1920s doll's house with dark rooms that smelled slightly musty. When I was a teenager, I helped my mother on her antiques stall, occasionally finding a bargain for myself.

The antiques trade has since been transformed by the internet. Auctions are online, so the exciting possibility of spotting a misidentified 18th-century dress or piece of Delftware at a local sale room is now virtually nil. If you find something in the attic, and have no idea of its value, you can simply look it up. And a slew of jokey television programmes pitting buyers against sellers, with the constant implication that it's acceptable to demand huge discounts, has done the trade no favours.

Another big change is the introduction of the word 'vintage' to describe anything that is old but not antique. The term migrated from fashion, where it has a longer history, and has glamorized what used to be dismissed as 'second-hand' or 'junk'. Vintage can cover anything and everything, from a potato masher with a painted wooden handle to an Ercol chair. This relatively young market for things that would

otherwise be discarded is a form of fashionable recycling that can only be good for the environment.

Vintage is the low-key, accessible end of the market, and often more affordable – though items that can be labelled mid-century modern, whether well-made and well-designed or not, command a premium. The term antique is usually taken to refer to anything that is more than a hundred years old, and this is an area of the market that some people find more intimidating – afraid they are going to be sold a dud and make an embarrassing mistake by paying too much.

Unless you are spending thousands, the best rule of thumb is that you will not regret buying something if you like it enough, particularly if it is something useful like a kitchen table. Even if you later discover that the scrubbed pine top didn't originally belong to the legs, as long as you are not planning to sell it on to make a profit, it doesn't really matter. It will still almost certainly be better made than any mass-produced equivalent, and probably cost less too. The same applies to dining chairs, which are particularly good value if you don't mind buying them singly and putting together a mismatched selection, and also chests of drawers – just check that the drawers fit properly and run reasonably smoothly – and all kinds of other common, serviceable pieces of furniture from the late 18th to the early 20th century.

Antique upholstered furnishings – sofas and armchairs – are more problematic. If the upholstery is not in good condition, you have to factor in the price of reupholstery, which is likely to be more than you will have paid for the piece of furniture itself. Use a good upholsterer, however, and you end up with something that has been well-constructed, and not held together with staples. New upholstered furniture made using traditional methods is expensive but, if you can afford it, a good investment.

The more confident you are, the more risks you can take, for example by buying at auction instead of from a shop. If you know exactly what you are getting – perhaps a particular make of china that you collect – you may decide you don't need to view. This is time-efficient but a lot less fun than going to have a look, when you can see and touch before deciding if you want something or not. After all, there are things no photograph can convey. The smell of mothballs in a drawer, or fabric, is almost impossible to get rid of. After viewing, you might decide to leave a bid. If you are competitive, the adrenaline of bidding for something in a room full of rival buyers can easily sweep you into paying more than you intended just for the satisfaction of 'winning'. All the above also applies to buying from any of the many online marketplaces.

Buying antiques should be a pleasure. Ask questions. Learn. Look until you start to feel confident about what you do and don't like. And make friends with dealers whose stock appeals. I may be biased, but I have always found most antique dealers to be generous with their knowledge, delightfully non-conformist, and often very kind. The best sort, those who buy things because they find them beautiful, intriguing, and evocative, love nothing more than passing them on to a buyer who appreciates them equally. And don't ask for huge discounts. It's actually quite rude.

PAGE 121 Antiques don't need to be perfect or 'right' to be desirable. The china-laden dresser in this tiny cottage kitchen is a 'marriage' of a Victorian sideboard and a later set of shelves, and the wall cupboard was in such bad condition that painting it buttercup yellow was an act of joyful rejuvenation rather than vandalism.

OPPOSITE If these chairs were as old as they look, they would be rare and valuable. In fact, they are early 20th-century fakes, quite robust enough for sitting on, and highly decorative in a bedroom that is otherwise plain.

PAGES 124–125 If an inherited antique feels too traditional for everyday, you can always break with convention and put it somewhere unexpected, like this grand 18th-century portrait in an attic guest room.

PAGE 125 ABOVE An antique knee-hole desk and leather-upholstered carver chair make a handsome home office.

PAGE 125 BELOW Some antiques are as practical as when they were first made, like this adjustable book rest, conveniently placed next to a comfortable chair.

OPPOSITE An 18th-century tallboy has exactly the right proportions for the rear reception room of an 18th-century London townhouse, as well as providing a lot of useful drawers. The two chairs are also 18th century.

ABOVE The only thing that is not antique in this country house bedroom is the brass wall light. Even the cushions and the regal red bedcover are made from old fabrics.

ABOVE An 18th-century table holds a collection of contemporary white ceramics, bringing together two very different versions of elegance. The style dissonance is visually striking and makes you look with fresh eyes at both old and new.

RIGHT This table can be extended with the insertion of an extra leaf, converting a library into a dining room – an antique both good-looking and versatile.

OPPOSITE Placing a single antique – here, an 18th-century drop-leaf table – in the midst of contemporary art and furnishings is always visually interesting. In this case, the antique is simple to the point of minimalism, but its wood is richly patinated in contrast with its pristine surroundings.

ABOVE LEFT There is charm as well as practicality in this arrangement of an old pine cupboard, a vintage lamp, and a bouquet of dried leaves in an antique enamel pitcher.

ABOVE RIGHT A grouping of 18th-century antiques that is harmonious and restrained – the blue of the pastel portrait picked up in the original, slightly scuffed paint of the table with its extending candle stands.

RIGHT Antique china is pretty, and so plentiful that it is easily affordable, especially if it has the odd chip or crack. The fact that it must be washed up by hand – most won't be robust enough for the dishwasher – is made up for by the pleasure of using it.

RIGHT An atmospheric selection of antique furnishings, including a rug and a brass chandelier, creating an impression that little has changed in this old house for generations. Only the painting strikes a more modern note.

BELOW The panelling and woodwork in the dining room of this early 18th-century townhouse replicate what was stripped out in the 1980s. The furnishings are all antique but of various periods, united by their dark wood. Filling a period room exactly to match its date makes it feel more museum than home.

OPPOSITE Antique furnishings and china enlivened by contemporary upholstery and fabrics in a country living room.

The Bedroom

With its embrace of fabrics, flowers, and nostalgia, there is a romance to English style that is well suited to bedrooms. Nancy Lancaster, doyenne of English country house style, had a formula that, more than half a century later, still feels definitive. Overnight guests at one of her country houses would be led upstairs to find a fire burning in the grate, fresh flowers, and a four-poster bed made up with down pillows and a silk eiderdown. As well as bedside tables with lamps, and an armoire for clothes, there would be a desk and a small sofa, a pair of armchairs or a day bed, such that these were private sitting rooms as much as bedrooms. There was central heating, and all had their own bathrooms – unheard of at a time when even a house as splendid as Cliveden only had two bathrooms to a floor.

This domestic luxury is now confined to the most expensive country house hotels. Nancy had big rooms to play with, and staff to launder bed linen and light fires. But some of her ideas can be translated, even on a less lavish scale. A bedroom, after all, is more than a place to sleep. Bedrooms are personal retreats – somewhere to escape for time alone, time to be quiet, to read, think, or try on outfits. Many bedrooms are not big enough for dressing tables and chests of drawers, let alone for desks and sofas, once the essentials of bedside tables and a wardrobe or fitted cupboards are slotted in, but the addition of a chair or a bookcase makes a bedroom feel more welcoming. If you also provide a radio, a kettle, and a tin of biscuits for your guests, the welcome will feel even warmer.

The bed is the focus, and the fabrics that dress and cover it the key to the decorative effect – a plain divan/box spring with a white duvet cover will not do. Like a grandfather clock in the hall, or a dresser in the kitchen, a four-poster bed is an icon of English style. These are the beds we read about as children, where princesses slept, or orphaned girls sent to live with distant relatives in draughty country houses. They belong in manor houses and stately homes, and furnish a thousand hotel honeymoon suites. The appeal is more than merely aesthetic. With their curtains and canopies, they offer little worlds of their own, a room within a room, cosy and contained, like a grown-up den.

Four-poster beds come in all shapes, sizes, and styles. Antique ones are pricey and often too narrow for modern ideas of comfort. The solution is usually to make a new bed frame for old posts. As for hangings, velvet and silk are harder to clean and care for than cotton, and what could be prettier, or more English, than a four-poster bed hung with flowery chintz, perhaps lined with a complementary sprig? Nor should you rule out the idea of a four-poster because you think a room too small. The drama of a bed that fills a room and skims the ceiling is a piece of interiors theatre not to be missed.

Less voluminous than a four-poster is a half-tester, which is effectively a deep pelmet with curtains. Then there are the various kinds of corona, with gathered fabric attached. If you cannot afford something original, there are less extravagant ways to make a decorative statement, whether with yards of muslin or second-hand curtains. Fabric can be looped over a bed from hooks in the ceiling. Or simply hang a drop of fabric on the wall behind the bed, perhaps an antique patchwork quilt, or panel of crewel work embroidery.

Bed linen is as important as hangings. It is hard to beat the indulgence of sliding into ironed and starched linen sheets. Freshly laundered cotton is a close second best. But, a bit like that fire that won't light itself, ironing double sheets or duvet covers, as well as pillowcases, is not something many people have time for. It is almost worth it, but if you can hang them out on a washing line, in sunshine and a breeze, you can get away without ironing sheets, even linen ones. Vintage or antique linen sheets are excellent value if you can find them in good condition. Check them by holding them up to the light to see if and where the fabric has worn thin. A bedspread on top, whether of a duvet, or sheets and blankets, makes a bed look finished.

Unless you are fortunate enough to have a dressing room or walk-in wardrobe/closet, another essential is storage for clothes. As with kitchens, the most efficient use of limited space is fitted cupboards. In an old house, the obvious place for these is often the recesses on either side of a chimney breast. If possible, they should be made by a joiner to fit, with doors that match other woodwork in the house, be they panelled or planked. Old free-standing wardrobes, with their shades of Narnia, look tremendous but are often not deep enough to hang clothes on hangers on a rail. For clothes that don't need to be hung, straightforward pine, oak, or mahogany chests of drawers from the late 18th and 19th centuries are practical, good-looking, and so common that they are often better value than a new equivalent.

Your own bedroom is the room least likely to be seen by visitors, so is a room you decorate for your own pleasure and somewhere you can enjoy those possessions that are most personal, whether a one-eyed teddy bear or treasured photographs. For older children, it can be an important arena for self-expression. Ask any adult decorator, and they will tell you that their interest in interior design began with their childhood bedroom.

Teenage experimentation aside, restful colours and quiet patterns are naturally preferable in a bedroom to anything loud, bright, or clashing. This is also the place, if you have it nowhere else, where you might consider wallpaper, which has a softer, warmer feel than paint. More cocooning still is fabric, stretched on battens. Both allow the possibility of all-over pattern, for walls, curtains, and bed, which is known as decorating 'in the French style', though it looks charmingly English, particularly in a cottage setting. Bedrooms may also be the only rooms where you choose to have fitted carpet. The look I like best is called velvet pile, which has sometimes survived in houses that have not been redecorated since the 1930s. It is still available, expensive, but a good investment, its flat, matt surface in a neutral shade an ideal background for rugs.

The look I have described is soft and essentially feminine. But there is another thread of English style that favours a more austere, ascetic bedroom. It still requires the comfort of fabrics, but enjoys the contrast between a hard wood floor and a sheepskin rug, a simple brass bed and a thick quilted bedspread. Unlike a kitchen, hall, or living room, this is a room you are quite likely to have more than one of. While it is probably best not to swing too wildly between the boudoir and the dormitory, you will inevitably suit a bedroom's occupants.

Colours, patterns, and furnishings aside, it is important to remember that comfort in a bedroom applies to the whole environment. As the place where we sleep and are most vulnerable, a bedroom should feel as quiet, safe, and peaceful as possible, warm for going to bed and getting up, but not too hot in between times – far better to be cosy under the bedclothes, yet breathing cool air. Curtains are essential, or shutters, or blackout blinds, so that our bodies know it is time to sleep. And lighting needs to be flexible, gentle overall, but with good lights to read by.

PAGE 135 Laundered bed linen matched by white paintwork, white lampshades, off-white upholstery, and the palest fitted carpet make this bedroom look clean and fresh as a daisy. Faded antique fabrics pick up on the pink of the large check valance, and everything is arranged to be soothing and easy, from the plump pillows to the bedside tables big enough to accommodate a radio, an alarm clock, and a vase of flowers.

PAGE 136 This splendid four-poster bed in a large country house bedroom has been constructed around a pair of antique bedposts in order to be wide enough for modern tastes, and is hung with a gathered pelmet and a drop of the same fabric behind the headboard.

RIGHT Soft colours and fabrics, including an array of embroidered cushions and a deeply padded headboard, in a guest bedroom. Again, the white paint and white lamps look as pristine as the sheets and pillowcases.

ABOVE A simple attic bedroom layered with the tactile warmth of sheepskin rugs laid on top of a large, plain rug, and a knitted woollen throw covering the bed.

OPPOSITE The big, blowsy roses of old-fashioned chintz curtains are matched by botanical prints of roses and a flowery embroidered bedcover, all set off against walls of calming sky blue. Provided with plentiful books and a tea tray, you might decide to stay in bed all morning.

ABOVE LEFT A single divan/box spring bed tucked into a corner can double as a bedroom sofa with cushions propped against the walls.

ABOVE RIGHT A bed is the focus of any bedroom, and fabrics are the key to its decorative effect. The easiest and probably least expensive way to give a modern bed a bit of visual clout is to hang a length of fabric behind it, here a beautiful piece of antique ikat.

LEFT In a bedroom that is largely all white, it is the selection of vintage clothing hanging on coat pegs that introduces warmth – and also just happens to match the sleeping cat.

OPPOSITE Single iron bedsteads, of the sort that might once have lined up in a dormitory, are made sumptuous by mounded pillows, feather eiderdowns, and generous knitted blankets. Extra tables at the ends of the beds make up for the fact that there is only space for a shared bedside table.

PAGE 144 An old-fashioned four-poster bed with all the trimmings; curtains, swags, drapes, and tassel fringing. The classic centrepiece for a grand country house bedroom, and the kind of bed that would make you feel like a princess, or a duchess at the very least.

PAGE 145 More feminine than a simple drop of fabric, but less domineering than a four-poster, a half-moon corona of gathered and lined chintz gives a bed height and decorative emphasis.

ABOVE It is important to feel safe in a bedroom as a room where we are at our most vulnerable while asleep, and an enclosed bed, such as a box bed, offers just that sense of security. Dressed with layers of antique fabrics, this bed tucked into an alcove looks particularly snug.

OPPOSITE Decorating a bedroom using the same fabric to cover the walls, for the curtains, and here to upholster and dress the bed is known as decorating 'in the French style', although to me it looks more typically English.

OPPOSITE There is something particularly appealing about the presence of an upholstered armchair in a bedroom, like an invitation to spend time during the day in quiet, private contemplation. This farmhouse bedroom has space for two chairs and a stool, so you could even include a friend.

RIGHT Red, particularly a rich strawberry red, is one of the few strong colours that feels right in a bedroom, especially when used in small doses like this checked blanket throw and frilled and gathered lampshade.

BELOW LEFT In a tiny bedroom, the width of the bed itself, wall shelves above the bed offer a choice of reading matter and are an efficient use of space. Here, the warm reds of the bedcover and book spines are set against paintwork of gentle shell pink.

BELOW RIGHT A shaped and padded headboard glamorizes a simple divan/box spring and makes sitting up in bed more comfortable.

ABOVE A four-poster bed stripped of its hangings looks clean and graphic, though this one is made more decorative thanks to the charm of an old patchwork quilt. Matting is softened by a rug, and books and flowers always make a guest room feel welcoming.

LEFT Single beds look increasingly old-fashioned in a world dominated by ever more enormous doubles, but are a good choice for a guest bedroom, especially when you only have one friend coming to stay.

OPPOSITE It is unusual to have quite so many books in a bedroom, but they add interest and warmth to any room, and here the shelving provides a window alcove that is the perfect place for a dressing table.

OPPOSITE An old iron bedstead feels just right in this cottage bedroom tucked under the eaves, any whiff of austerity banished by the lacy white pillowcases and quilted floral bedspread.

ABOVE A four-poster particularly well-dressed with floral chintz lined with a monochrome sprig. The addition of a sofa at the foot of the bed provides an extra dose of comfort and convenience.

OPPOSITE Under the steeply beamed roof of a medieval cottage, this pared-back bedroom with its bare, painted floorboards and sparse furnishings is an invitation to leap into the warm embrace of a bed piled with pillows and topped with a thickly quilted patchwork bedspread.

ABOVE The muted colours of antique fabrics, here a quilted bedspread and a needlework cushion on a vintage armchair, are matched by the original paint of a Victorian pine chest of drawers in the guest bedroom of a 16th-century house.

RIGHT A splendid antique wooden bedstead presides over this small, panelled bedroom. Like fabric used as wallcovering, wooden panelling makes a room feel insulated and cosy.

Fabrics

Life would be uncomfortable without woven fabrics – little wonder our distant ancestors had to come up with something other than animal skins. Clothing is essential, but a home without fabrics is equally unthinkable. Fabrics cushion our bodies and provide warmth and softness, as well as delighting our eyes with contrasts and harmonies of colour and pattern, and appealing to our sense of touch with textures from the sheen of glazed chintz to the shadowy down of velvet. They also absorb sound, protecting our ears from clatter and echo. In an English interior, fabrics take centre stage.

The fact that we can be so generous, wasteful even, with fabrics is a relatively new phenomenon. Before the invention of machines that could spin and weave, fabric manufacture, whether silk, wool, linen, hemp, or cotton, was painstaking, time-consuming, and skilled. Fabrics, especially those that could not be made at home, were expensive and treasured, reused and upcycled until they disintegrated. When Henry VIII ordered a set of tapestries for Hampton Court, the money he spent on them could have bought two fully equipped battleships.

English style gobbles up a lot of fabric. Curtains are essential to the look, especially in living rooms and bedrooms. Equally important are upholstered furnishings, which may include stools, ottomans, club fenders, and bedheads. Loose/slip covers on sofas and armchairs have a particularly English informality, especially when they don't fit snugly. And no English chair or sofa is complete without its complement of fat, down-filled cushions. Then there are wall hangings, bed hangings, bedspreads, tablecloths, and framed needlework.

Of the myriad fabrics used to adorn a room, chintz is most closely associated with English interiors. The word derives from the Hindi for 'variegated', and was used to describe the calicoes printed and painted with floral and tree-of-life designs that were produced in Hyderabad and imported to Europe from the 16th century. This too was costly and highly prized. Then at the end of the 18th century everything changed. A series of inventions kicked off the Industrial Revolution, making England the workshop of the world, its cotton mills mass-producing a washable, durable, pretty fabric that was affordable. Since when, printed cotton in all its charming, decorative variety has never entirely gone out of fashion, and the flowers that wreathed those early designs, their inspiration taken from Mughal art, have become the most evergreen of all.

John Fowler loved floral chintz for the way it brought the garden indoors, an impulse that remains one of the abiding characteristics of English style. Today, there is a whole herbaceous border of designs to choose from: hydrangeas, roses, delphiniums, tulips, fuchsias, geraniums, peonies, poppies, sweet peas, carnations, foxgloves, and pansies, scattered, bunched, or entwined on cottons and linens to be hung at windows, stretched across sofas, or used to cover cushions. Every year, fabric companies produce a bouquet of new florals, but the oldest remain some of the best, especially those taken from antique originals, designs that seem impervious to fashion, such as 'Bowood', which John Fowler copied from a fabric found in a bedroom of Bowood House, or 'Bennison Roses', copied from a 19th-century piece by antique dealer and decorator Geoffrey Bennison.

While piffling compared with the cost of a battleship, the best and most beautiful new fabrics are far from cheap, especially in the amounts required for a pair of full-length curtains. Blinds use a fraction of the amount of material, and may be more appropriate in kitchens and bathrooms and for small windows, but curtains, their gathered folds framing the architecture of a window, shifting in a summer breeze, or drawn against the chill of draughts in winter, are more typically English. And because of our cold, damp climate, they are usually lined, and often interlined, such that they drape in plump, rounded folds when drawn back, and offer insulation as effective as double glazing when closed.

As with so many aspects of English style, fabrics do not have to be new, and those with a certain amount of wear and fading look better than anything too crisp or bright. Because there is a substantial discount for second-hand as opposed to newly made curtains, you are able to afford something of much higher quality. However, it is likely that your options will be limited, although this has the advantage that you are less vulnerable to the paralysis of too much choice, and endless leafing through sample books, dithering over what will look best. Size is obviously an issue – it's no good falling in love with a pair of old curtains that would only cover half your window, though if the discrepancy is not too great, you can lengthen and widen them by adding borders of a plain or contrasting fabric.

Second-hand curtains are practical and affordable. But antique fabrics of all kinds add atmosphere and history to a room, whether a piece of wool needlework upholstering a stool, a paisley shawl covering a table, or an old plaid blanket draped over the back of a sofa. While some antique fabrics are robust enough for regular use – linen and hemp sheets, for example, or quilted bedspreads, or damask tablecloths and napkins – others are more fragile. It is always tempting to use something beautiful rather than putting it away in a drawer. But fabrics are prone to wear out, and decay in sunlight. They have always been recycled, hence making patchwork from worn-out dresses, but there is a difficult choice between preservation and enjoyment. Damaged items, such as a moth-eaten tapestry, tattered toile de Jouy bed hangings, or a disintegrating item of clothing can be cut up and given new life as cushions with a clear conscience. If something is perfect and rare, shortening its life by use feels less excusable. A compromise might be to keep it in a drawer and bring it out for special occasions.

The scope for mixing patterns, colours, and styles of fabric is infinite and, for those who are not professional decorators, often a question of trial and error. Chintz may be quintessential, but this is where English decoration can be at at its most inclusive, by combining the old with the new, the plain with the fancy, the rough with the smooth, and also by using fabrics from different countries, cultures, and continents. Just as we have always carpeted our floors with rugs from Turkey and the Middle East, so we have collected and valued fabrics from around the world, whether painted Chinese silks, embroidered suzanis from Central Asia, block-printed calicoes from India, or lengths of African kuba cloth. Adding these to a room is like pepping up a rich stew with a sprinkling of spices, and as English as making a grandfather clock in imitation of Japanese red lacquer, or embellishing a teapot with images of Greek goddesses.

PAGE 157 This delicious meeting of pattern and colour – a contemporary wallpaper, with antique glazed chintz curtains – adorns a bathroom, a room that would originally have been a bedroom in a small terraced townhouse. The gilded chair has been stripped back to its hessian and horsehair underwear.

OPPOSITE Two lovely examples of upcycling by Nest Design – an updated and upgraded version of net curtains using antique embroidered table linen, and curtains made from old blankets trimmed with a border of antique velvet and broderie anglaise.

LEFT There is something perennially pleasing to the eye about the combination of stripes or checks with a floral chintz – here, cushions on a Victorian chaise longue. Second-hand curtains, which are too long for the window, have been allowed to puddle on the floor.

OPPOSITE ABOVE LEFT The shelves of an armoire hold piles of vintage eiderdowns and there is a particularly pretty one spread on the bed. Curtains are a vintage printed linen and even the chair cushion is made using old fabric.

OPPOSITE ABOVE RIGHT The colours of printed antique linen fade in a particularly appealing way, and the fabric usually remains strong enough to be practical for use as curtains and cushions.

OPPOSITE BELOW LEFT A selection of antique fabrics, including quilted bedspreads. These are plentiful, as every 19th-century household had at least one, as well as usable and warm. The quilting is hand stitched and represents hours of work.

OPPOSITE BELOW RIGHT Antique glazed chintz curtains, antique printed cotton bed hangings, their floral pattern so faded it has almost disappeared, and a bedspread that is probably 18th century in a country house bedroom.

PAGES 162–163 A living room where old and new fabrics happily coexist, their colours reflected in the peony print of the linen curtains. The fabric covering the screen is modern but looks antique due to its faded, patchy colours.

PAGE 164 A simple, modern divan/box spring made lovely by its dressing of fabrics; a plain valance in a muted linen damask, an antique fringed and embroidered bedspread, and a drop of hand-embroidered fabric creating a simple backdrop and canopy looped up between the wall and a ceiling beam.

PAGE 165 ABOVE LEFT Jewel colours and sheepskin rugs warm up an all-white bedroom. A large framed scarf design and two oversized cushions play the same visual role as a bedhead.

PAGE 165 ABOVE RIGHT An antique bed that benefits from a wooden bedhead and the extra decorative emphasis of an embroidered cloth hung behind it. The bedspread is an old suzani.

PAGE 165 BELOW There are some patterns that never go out of fashion. Blue and white stripes of all varieties have a perennial charm and look particularly crisp in a white room.

LEFT A guest bedroom where textiles have been allowed to congregate in a layering of pattern and colour that includes leopard print, crewel work, and chintz.

OPPOSITE Another room of multiple pattern, rainbow colours, and a profound sense of comfort, all provided by fabrics and including a vintage silk lampshade with bobble fringing.

ABOVE If you are lucky enough to find a pair of antique or second-hand curtains complete with matching pelmet, you can create a home-made half-tester bed, as here. In this instance, there was enough glazed chintz left over to upholster the headboard to match. A pleated silk lampshade in cream casts a soft and flattering light.

RIGHT In the 1980s, the fashion for swagged and draped curtains got a bit out of hand, and this kind of complicated curtain treatment was popping up in cottages and swamping small windows. In a room with grand proportions and windows to match, the effect is much more appropriate and visually pleasing, though not something to be attempted by an amateur.

The Bathroom

There has been a tendency in recent years, inspired by super-slick hotels, for bathrooms to look and feel increasingly like wipe-clean laboratories, everything smooth, hard, and shiny. Flooring slides seamlessly into shower areas, mirrored cabinets uninterrupted by handles are set flush into walls above basins without lips, and single taps like minimalist sculptures offer no helpful cues on how to use them. These sleek capsules work best in new houses where plumbing is incorporated in the build, and make efficient use of limited space in urban apartments. But they are the antithesis of an English bathroom.

Bathrooms came late to English domestic architecture. Although by the end of the 19th century luxurious houses were fitted with flushing lavatories encased in panelled mahogany, and cast-iron bathtubs – some even incorporating showers with a battery of pipes squirting jets of hot water – for most people a tin tub filled from kettles heated on the kitchen range and an outdoor privy remained the norm. Today, in houses that pre-date 1900, bathrooms usually occupy former bedrooms, meaning they are big enough to swing cats in, and always have at least one window.

More space allows scope for bulkier sanitaryware, in particular the free-standing roll-top bathtub. With their decorative feet, these tubs have the presence of a large piece of furniture and look splendid placed in front of a window or fireplace, like majestic boats lying at anchor. What they do not afford is anywhere to put soap or shampoo, requiring the addition of a bath rack, a shelf, or a side table.

There are reproduction roll-top bathtubs available as well as antique ones. The same applies to washbasins, which can be found at most reclamation yards, as well as in ranges of 'heritage' sanitaryware. Designs dating from the early 20th century to the 1950s are practical as well as handsome. Most have two taps/faucets, integral soap dishes, space for a toothbrush mug, and a plug on a chain. The taps/faucets are easy to use, and the basins are wide and deep enough

such that you can splash your face with cold water without watering the floor. An alternative is to have basins fitted into a piece of antique furniture like an old washstand. There are thousands of contemporary variations on the washbasin theme, but most are less user-friendly than their traditional antecedents.

As for the lavatory, you could opt for a genuine antique, with a high-level cistern and a chain. These often have bowls decorated as though they belonged to a china dinner service, and stirring names such as 'Excelsior' and 'Invictas'. Or you could do as Nancy Lancaster did and fit a *chaise percée*, an antique chair with a seat that lifts, set over the bowl and disguising it as a piece of furniture. Far simpler is to fit a wooden seat with a lid – appealingly old-fashioned and far nicer to sit on than plastic.

The aim with all these choices is to make a bathroom look furnished rather than fitted. Showers are tucked into corners, and tiling is kept to a minimum. There may be wallpaper, and curtains at the window, fitted carpet, or floorboards and a rug. The mirror above the basin is an old one, and there are pictures on the walls. In a small bathroom there might only be space for a chair, but in bigger rooms you could have a cabinet displaying shells, a small chest of drawers for toiletries, or a rack holding magazines. It can be as plain or as pretty as you like, but what it should not be is clinical.

PAGE 171 The bigger a bathroom, the more scope there is for furnishings – here, an antique linen press and an armchair, plus rugs and pictures. Every roll-top bathtub requires some kind of rack or shelf for the soap. This one has both.

RIGHT In a big and well-ventilated bathroom, there is no reason not to have wallpaper, nor should it need to be sealed. This bathroom is glamorized by a magnificent scenic wallpaper with an appropriately watery theme.

BELOW LEFT Painted boards make practical flooring that is not too cold for bare feet. In this farmhouse bathroom, they mirror the planked ceiling with its original limewash.

BELOW RIGHT This curvy roll-top tub benefits from its own mini console table with a bowl for holding soap and sponge.

OPPOSITE A roll-top bathtub has unrivalled splendour, but a cast-iron enamelled corner bathtub, its sides panelled with wood, its edges lined with a protective frieze of tiling, is a pleasure to use, with taps/faucets at one end that can be turned on and off with your toes as you lie back for a good soak. Pot plants like these pelargoniums look good in a bathroom, and often thrive in the warmth and moisture.

ABOVE In this bathroom, once a bedroom, there is a wonderful dissonance between the historic interior architecture, with its centuries of wear and tear, and the bright green vintage bathroom suite, which looks as though it has time-travelled from another century.

OPPOSITE An antique tin tub, its plumbing hidden by a wooden plinth, is perfectly at home in this panelled interior. An old glass-fronted chemist's cabinet makes for appropriate storage, although it is almost entirely filled with decorative pieces.

LEFT Roll-top bathtubs, both old and new, have feet and exteriors that can be painted, here to match the wooden wall panelling.

BELOW LEFT It would be prohibitively expensive to use an expanse of antique Delft tiling in a bathroom, but just four tiles, all with different designs, make a charming splashback for a vintage washbasin.

BELOW RIGHT A downstairs lavatory, a small room that is visited rather than lingered in, is an opportunity for bold colour and decoration – in this case, buttercup yellow paint and a grid of black and white engravings.

OPPOSITE This room has been decorated by artist Adam Calkin with a painted frieze and colourful geometric floor such that you hardly notice it is a bathroom. The lavatory is disguised as an antique chair and the basin discreetly fitted into the top of a console table.

OPPOSITE Contrasts are always visually exciting. In another bathroom in an old house that has retained its vintage 1930s bathroom fittings, both walls and floor have been stripped bare, while the rose pink ceramic of the magnificently solid bathtub is smooth, unblemished, and looks as good as new.

BELOW Fitted carpet makes a bathroom feel luxurious and, when it continues seamlessly from an adjacent bedroom, more like an extension of that room rather than somewhere strictly reserved for ablutions.

PAGE 180 With its bathtub placed centre stage, its matching pair of washbasins, each with a grand antique mirror hung above, and its antique furnishings, including a stool, chair, and dressing table, this bathroom is the height of elegance.

PAGE 181 Pictures can furnish a room in the same way as books. The charm of this small bathroom, with its washbasin neatly set into the window embrasure, is largely due to the botanical prints that line its walls. Glass is an old-fashioned alternative to tiles for protecting walls around a bathtub.

OPPOSITE Fabrics and furnishings, in addition to bathtub, basin, and towels, can give a bathroom as much character as any other room in the house. Here, the red stripe of antique linen towels is picked up by the stripe of the lampshade.

RIGHT This bathroom is partially separated from the bedroom by a half-wall, and carpeting and wallpaper flow from one into the other. A radiator cover under the window provides the necessary shelf for soap and bath oils.

BELOW RIGHT Pretty wallpaper instantly softens the effect of hard surfaces in a bathroom and here makes a good match with the marble used to surround the bathtub and washbasin.

OPPOSITE Fitting a bathroom into an early 18th-century house requires some architectural sensitivity. A centrally placed roll-top bathtub, affording a view of chimney tops, leaves walls free, which is important if there is original panelling. Here it had been stripped out, but a Victorian fireplace remained, now flanked by floor-to-ceiling cupboards big enough to enclose a shower and lavatory.

ABOVE Another bathroom in an early 18th-century house, this time on the top floor and fitted under the steep slope of the roof. The original woodwork has been preserved and painted a dramatic deep plum, against which the white sanitaryware positively sparkles.

RIGHT Wallpaper, a picture, an antique chair, and a row of old bottles – simple ingredients that transform a small bathroom from utilitarian to decorated.

Collections

English style rejoices in the unnecessary and decorative – ranked on mantelpieces and kitchen dressers, set out on windowsills and side tables, arrayed on shelves behind the glass doors of cabinets, grouped on walls – collections of things, whether mocha ware mugs or brass candlesticks, architectural prints or Delft tiles, all can be happily accommodated.

The urge to collect is universal, tapping into ancient hunter-gatherer instincts. Children collect conkers and particular kinds of toy. As adults, the urge to seek and acquire doesn't necessarily fade, though the objects of desire tend to become more sophisticated. Collections are part of what make an English interior personal and expressive and, when they get out of hand, eccentric.

Like pictures, books are a staple of English interiors, and have a place in every room from the downstairs lavatory to the attic bedroom. A wall of bookshelves is a handsome addition to a room, and has the same enveloping, insulating effect as panelling. Whether ordered alphabetically, by subject, or by size and colour, the barcode stripes of book spines are as pleasing visually as their titles are intriguing. Their presence in a room goes beyond appearances, offering a world of stories, images, ideas, and knowledge, sending out signals about the interests and tastes of their owner.

Books belong in bookcases, from which they often escape to form stacks and towers on tables, desks, and the floor, but the display of other collected things may need more thought. Related items look better when gathered together. Staffordshire figures come to life as a crowd, and glass has more aesthetic punch when grouped somewhere it can catch the light, such as in a window embrasure. Objects that are unassuming singly can have impact en masse; an arrangement of hand mirrors hung on a wall, perhaps, or a cluster of coloured bud vases. And if things belong to the same decorative family they will sit well together, even if they are from different periods and in different styles. You can fill a kitchen dresser with blue and white china, putting 18th-century Wedgwood with 19th-century Spode, transferware with spongeware, throw a few Cornishware stripes into the mix, and make a pleasing arrangement.

The same principle applies to pictures. A big oil painting will stand its ground alone on a wall or above a fireplace, but smaller drawings, prints, or watercolours have more clout when closely hung. This is a good way to corral family photographs, covering a wall with a tessellation of faces. In smaller rooms choose a theme, such as nautical watercolours, or shell prints for a bathroom. Botanical and flower pictures are restful and pretty for a bedroom, and look particularly smart in a grid if they are uniformly framed.

If you collect big things like vintage bicycles or 19th-century trunks, you will run out of space to show them off. Small items, on the other hand, need containment to protect them from damage and dust. What you need is some kind of glass-fronted cabinet. This can look poised and elegant if the arrangement is sparse, and stylish if you paint the interior a strong colour like peacock blue or aubergine. If you go for a more dense selection of objects, perhaps mingling more than one collection – tea bowls with woven silk ribbons, and doll's house chairs, for example – you can recreate the excitement of discovery you get in old-fashioned museums where items are crowded into dimly lit cases. While some collections can be enjoyed from the other side of the room, others need close and attentive scrutiny.

PAGE 186 An 18th-century Welsh dresser holds a magnificent selection of 18th-century mocha ware plates, each one different, but united by their earthy colours and the technique by which their mottled, dappled glaze was achieved.

OPPOSITE Another dresser, arranged with a mix of antique china of different dates and styles. Blue and white china predominates, and helps to create a visual theme.

When a collection is used and not purely decorative – such as these vintage and antique beads and bracelets, including pieces in coral and amber – it is good to display it somewhere accessible, as on this table by a bedroom window.

OPPOSITE This crowd of antique china, arranged on specially made wall shelves at the dining end of a kitchen, is nearly all pink or lustre or both. Contemporary pieces on the bottom shelf echo and reinforce the colour scheme.

ABOVE Many things look better en masse than singly. It can be hard to find a way to display family photographs without dotting them around. Gathering them in a single, tight grouping, as on the wall in this breakfast room, is a stylish solution.

OPPOSITE Small collections can be fitted into small spaces – here, creamware drainers hung on the wall above a kitchen sink. Arranged in a column, they look more like an artwork than kitchen utensils.

ABOVE LEFT Finding an appropriate room for a particular collection helps to integrate it, such as shells in a bathroom. Small things are always better behind glass, where they are safe and don't need to be dusted.

ABOVE RIGHT A single china swan makes a fraction of the impact that this flock of them does gathered on the top of a cabinet in a cottage bedroom.

RIGHT The oddest things start to look interesting when there are more than one or two of them, in this case old alarm clocks ranged along the radiator shelf in a hall.

RIGHT There is something profoundly eccentric, as well as visually arresting, about a bathroom given over almost entirely to a mass gathering of religious imagery – the result of assiduous and prolonged hunting. The framed images are 19th-century pressed paper mourning cards sent to notify friends and family of a death.

LEFT One way to accommodate a large collection, here of 18th-century engravings, is to pack them in tightly – not easy to do, but when attention is paid to scale and balance, the effect is very pleasing.

BELOW Collecting books feels more virtuous than self-indulgent, and a wall of them with their variegated colourful spines always looks handsome.

OPPOSITE Jim Ede of Kettle's Yard made an art form of displaying *objets trouvés*. Pebbles, feathers, shells, birds' eggs, and tiny bones are all waiting to be found and have a beauty that can be appreciated at leisure if you bring them home.

OPPOSITE ABOVE LEFT
The narrow entrance hall of
a townhouse is the ideal place
to hang architectural prints,
where they are seen at close
quarters and can be studied
in all their fine detail.

OPPOSITE ABOVE RIGHT
Small convex mirrors hung one
above the other, each offering a
condensed and slightly different
view of the same room.

OPPOSITE BELOW LEFT
These small classical busts fill
a mantelpiece and have started
to creep up the walls on either
side of the mirror.

OPPOSITE BELOW RIGHT
Pastille burners and tea sets, all
modelled to look like cottages,

make a series of miniature
village streets gathered
together on a set of shelves.

ABOVE LEFT Dozens of broken
clay pipes found in the gardens
of a 17th-century house now
fill a bowl and invite closer
examination.

ABOVE RIGHT Vintage bud
vases, which can be bought for
a few pounds, look insignificant
singly, but make a row of
glowing colour when lined up.
Beneath them, bead necklaces
dangle from hooks.

RIGHT Old printing blocks,
their carved images dark with
ink, make a fascinating and
graphic pictorial display.

Sources

ARCHITECTURAL SALVAGE

Lassco
Brunswick House
30 Wandsworth Road
London SW8 2LG
+44 (0)20 7394 2100
www.lassco.co.uk
*A huge stock of everything from
fireplaces to floors to stained
glass, panelling, and staircases.
Visit their website for details of
their branches in Bermondsey
and Oxfordshire.*

Norfolk Reclaim Ltd
Helhoughton Road
Fakenham
Norfolk NR21 7DY
+44 (0)1328 864743
www.norfolkreclaim.co.uk
*Reclaimed building materials
including bricks, pantiles and
paving, plus architectural
antiques and furnishings.*

Oak Beam UK
Ermin Farm
Cricklade Road
Cirencester
Gloucestershire GL7 5PN
+44 (0)1285 869222
www.oakbeamuk.com
*Reclaimed oak beams salvaged
from Britain and France.*

www.oldoakfloor.com
*Antique oak floorboards
from France.*

Retrouvius
1016 Harrow Road
London NW10 5NS
+44 (0)20 8960 6060
www.retrouvius.com
*Fabulous stock of reclaimed
and repurposed antique and
vintage furnishings and fittings.*

Wells Reclamation
Coxley
Wells
Somerset BA5 1RQ
+44 (0)1749 677087
www.wellsreclamation.com
*Five and a half acres of
architectural salvage, reclaimed
building materials, and antique
and vintage furnishings.*

BATHROOMS

**Antique Bathrooms
of Ivybridge**
Erme Bridge Works
Ermington Road
Ivybridge
Devon PL21 9DE
+44 (0)1752 698250
www.antiquebaths.com
*Reconditioned antique bathtubs,
plus reproduction ranges.*

Balineum
www.balineum.co.uk
*Online bathroom fittings
and accessories, and a choice
of pretty hand-painted tiles.*

C P Hart
213 Newnham Terrace
Hercules Road
London SE1 7DR
+44 (0)20 7902 5250
and branches
www.cphart.co.uk
Inspiring bathroom showrooms.

Stiffkey Bathrooms
89 Upper St Giles Street
Norwich NR2 1AB
+44 (0)1603 627850
www.stiffkeybathrooms.com
*Antique sanitaryware, plus
their own range of reproduction
bathroom accessories.*

The Water Monopoly
10/14 Lonsdale Road
London NW6 6RD
+44 (0)20 7624 2636
www.thewatermonopoly.com
*Opulent period bathtubs,
basins, and fittings.*

FABRICS

Bennison Fabrics
16 Holbein Place
London SW1W 8NL
+44 (0)20 7730 8076
www.bennisonfabrics.com
*Chintzes, florals, stripes,
and damasks inspired by
antique originals.*

Chelsea Textiles
7 Walton Street
London SW3 2JD
+44 (0)20 7584 0111
www.chelseatextiles.com
*Embroidered cottons, delicate
prints, linens, silks, and voiles
with an 18th-century feel.*

Colefax and Fowler
110 Fulham Road
London SW3 6HU
+44 (0)20 7244 7427
www.colefax.com
*Quintessentially English
fabrics and wallpapers, but
also excellent for checks,
ginghams, and stripes.*

GP & J Baker
Unit 10 Ground Floor
Design Centre East
Chelsea Harbour Design Centre
London SW10 OXF
+44 (0)20 7351 7760
www.gpjbaker.co.uk
*Comprehensive range of fabrics
including both traditional and
contemporary.*

Ian Mankin
269/271 Wandsworth Bridge Road
London SW6 2TX
+44 (0)20 7722 0997
www.ianmankin.co.uk
*Natural fabrics, including
unbleached linens, butter
muslin, and striped tickings.*

Lewis & Wood
105–106 First Floor
Design Centre East
Chelsea Harbour
London SW10 0XF
+44 (0)20 7751 4554
www.lewisandwood.co.uk
*At the grander end of decorating
with large-scale fabrics and
wallpapers.*

Robert Kime
190–192 Ebury Street,
London SW1W 8UP
+44 (0)20 7831 6066
www.robertkime.com
*Best of British decorators in the
English style, with a gorgeous
range of fabrics and wallpapers,
and a choice selection of antiques.*

Russell & Chapple
30–31 Store Street
London WC1E 7QE
+44 (0)20 7836 7521
www.randc.net
*Artist's canvas in various
weights, jutes, fine muslin,
deckchair canvas, and
hessian sacking.*

Susan Deliss
www.susandeliss.com
*Gorgeous bespoke fabrics,
including antique and exotic
embroideries, cushions, and
ikat lampshades.*

Tinsmiths
8a High Street
Ledbury
Herefordshire HR8 1DS
+44 (0)1531 632083
www.tinsmiths.co.uk
*Handwoven and printed
textiles, including washed
linens, African indigo cottons,
and Indian block prints, plus
lighting, studio ceramics,
blankets, and cushions.*

Thornback & Peel
www.thornbackandpeel.co.uk
*Fresh screen-printed cottons,
including their instantly
recognizable 'Pigeon & Jelly'
and 'Rabbit & Cabbage' designs.*

ANTIQUE FABRICS

Katharine Pole
+44 (0)774 761 6692
www.katharinepole.com
*Wonderful selection of antique
textiles, including toiles, plain
linens, and stripes.*

Mason Taylor London
@masontaylorlondon
su.mason@yahoo.co.uk
*Mother and daughter Su and
Romilly Mason offer French
antique linens, workwear
and textiles on Instagram.*

Talent for Textiles
www.talentfortextiles.com
Contact Caroline Bushell on
+44 (0)1404 45901 or Linda
Clift on +44 (0)1305 264914.
*Organizers of antique textiles
fairs, bringing together dealers
from all over the country in a
series of attractive locations.*

FITTINGS

Brass Foundry Castings
+44 (0)1424 893158
www.brasscastings.co.uk
*More than 800 brass and
foundry castings for furniture,
doors, and clocks reproduced
from 17th- to 20th-century
originals, available online
or mail order only.*

Clayton Munroe
+44 (0)1803 865700
www.claytonmunroe.com
*Traditional handles, iron
hinges, and latches, available
mail order only.*

FURNITURE –
CONTEMPORARY

The Conran Shop
81 Fulham Road
London SW3 6RD
+44 (0)207 589 7401
and branches
www.conranshop.co.uk
*Tasteful modern furniture that
mixes well with antiques and
looks good in older buildings.*

Heal's
196 Tottenham Court Road
London W1T 7LQ
+44 (0)20 7636 1666
and branches
www.heals.com
*Good-quality
contemporary furniture.*

MADE
www.made.com
*Contemporary furniture sourced
directly from the makers.*

OKA
www.okadirect.com
*Good-quality, mid-price
furnishings in contemporary
and traditional styles.*

SCP
135–139 Curtain Road
London EC2A 3BX
+44 (0)20 7739 1869
www.scp.co.uk
*Manufacturer and retailer
of the work of contemporary
British designers, including
Matthew Hilton.*

FURNITURE –
ANTIQUE, VINTAGE
AND TRADITIONAL

After Noah
121–122 Upper Street
London N1 1QP
+44 (0)20 73594281
www.afternoah.com
*An appealing mix of antique,
vintage, and contemporary
furnishings, including cast-iron
beds, lighting, and toys.*

Alfies Antiques Market
13–25 Church Street
London NW8 8DT
+44 (0)20 7723 6066
www.alfiesantiques.com
*Vintage, retro, and antique
furnishings, and a good source
of mid-century modern.*

Bed Bazaar
Old Railway Station
Station Road
Framlingham
Suffolk IP13 9EE
+44 (0)1728 723756
www.bedbazaar.co.uk
*Antique metal and wooden
beds and handmade
mattresses to order.*

Berdoulat
8 Margaret's Buildings
Bath BA1 2LP
www.berdoulat.co.uk
*Specialists in period buildings
and restoration projects, with
a small range of kitchenware,
tableware, decorative products,
and bespoke furniture.*

Crowman Antiques
54 Northgate Street
Devizes
Wiltshire SN10 1JJ
+44 (0)1380 725548
*English country furniture,
treen, and silver.*

The French House
The Warehouse
North Lane
Huntington
York YO32 9SU
+44 (0)1904 400561
www.thefrenchhouse.co.uk
*French antiques, from armoires
to birdcages and bathtubs.*

George Smith
587–589 Kings Road
London SW6 2EH
+44 (0)20 7384 1004
www.georgesmith.com
*Capacious and relaxed
traditional sofas and armchairs.*

Joanna Booth
+44 (0)20 7352 8998
www.joannabooth.co.uk
*Early and rare antiques,
including sculpture and
tapestries.*

Max Rollitt
Yavington Barn
Lovington Lane
Avington
Hampshire SO21 1DA
+44 (0)1962 791124
www.maxrollitt.com
(Showroom open by appointment)
*Fine antiques as well as bespoke
furniture design.*

Robert Young Antiques
68 Battersea Bridge Road
London SW11 3AG
+44 (0)20 7228 7847
www.robertyoungantiques.com
*Fine English furniture and
folk art.*

Spencer Swaffer Antiques
30 High Street
Arundel
West Sussex BN18 9AB
+44 (0)1903 882132
www.spencerswaffer.com
*Pretty shop with glamorous
stock of decorative antiques.*

Wessex Beds
The Old Glove Works
Percombe
Near Stoke-sub-Hamdon
Somerset TA14 6RD
+44 (0)1935 829147
www.wessexbeds.co.uk
*Extensive selection of antique
beds, including brass bedsteads.*

FLOORING

Alternative Flooring Company
www.alternativeflooring.com
*Coir, seagrass, sisal, and jute
floor coverings, as well as
vibrantly patterned wool
carpets. Rugs made to size.*

Bernard Dru Oak
www.oakfloor.co.uk
*Specialists in the supply and
installation of English oak
flooring and parquet design,
made from wood from the
company's own woodlands.*

Crucial Trading
www.crucial-trading.com
*All types of natural floorings,
most of which can also be
ordered as rugs bound with
cotton, linen, or leather.*

Delabole Slate
www.delaboleslate.co.uk
*Riven slate or slate slabs
quarried in Cornwall and
suitable for work surfaces,
landscaping, fireplaces,
and flooring.*

Farnham Antique Carpets
The Old Parsonage
Church Street
Crondall
Surrey GU10 5QQ
44 (0)1252 851215
www.farnhamantiquecarpets.com
*Antique rug specialists
offering a full service including
restoration and advice, plus
a big selection of rugs for sale.*

**Robert Stephenson and
Giuseppe Giannini**
1 Elystan Street
London SW3 3NT
44 (0)20 7225 2343
www.robertstephenson.co.uk
*Antique rugs from all over
the world, including a lovely
selection of kilims, plus a
specialist restoration and
valuation service.*

Roger Oates Design
www.rogeroates.com
*All kinds of natural floorings,
including chunky abaca, plus
flat-weave rugs and runners
in chic stripes of gorgeous
colour combinations.*

Rush Matters
www.rushmatters.co.uk
*Rush matting made with
English rushes, also baskets
and rush seating for chairs.*

Solid Floor
61 Paddington Street
London W1U 4JD
+44 (0)20 7486 4838
www.solidfloor.co.uk
*Quality wooden floors made
from sustainable timber.*

Woodworks by Ted Todd
London Design Centre
79 Margaret Street
London W1W 8TA
+44 (0)20 7495 6706
www.tedtodd.co.uk
*Reclaimed, new, and antique
timber flooring and joinery.*

HEATING

Bisque
Suite 200
Business Design Centre
52 Upper Street
London N1 0QH
www.bisque.co.uk
*Suppliers of classic fin
radiators.*

Jamb
95–97 Pimlico Road
London SW1W 8PH
+44 (0)20 7730 2122
and at
8525 Melrose Avenue
West Hollywood
CA 90069
United States
+1 310 315 3028
Very high-quality reproduction antique fireplaces, also antique fireplaces, reproduction lighting, and an extremely smart selection of antique furnishings.

The Windy Smithy
+44 (0)7866 241783
www.windysmithy.co.uk
Bespoke wood-burning stoves.

FINISHING TOUCHES

Fabulous Vintage Finds
www.fabulousvintagefinds.co.uk
Jess Walton and her husband travel around France finding furniture and decorative items to sell, available online and from pop-up shops and markets.

Pentreath & Hall
17 Rugby Street
London WC1N 3QT
+44 (0)20 7430 2526
www.pentreath-hall.com
Irresistible homewares.

Perfect English Stuff
www.perfectenglishstuff.com
Blatant self-promotion – online antiques store selling decorative antique and vintage items found by three generations of my family: my mother Margery Byam Shaw, me, and my daughter Elizabeth Kemp.

Phillips & Cheers
www.phillipsandcheers.com
Cushions and lampshades made using vintage floral fabrics.

Ryder & Hope
30 Broad Street
Lyme Regis
Dorset DT7 3QE
+44 (0)1297 443304
www.ryderandhope.com
Stylish, contemporary artisan crafts.

Tat London
www.tat-london.co.uk
Lovely online selection of vintage and antique pieces.

KITCHENS

deVOL
36 St John's Square
London EC1V 4JJ
+44 (0)20 3879 7900
www.devolkitchens.co.uk
Handcrafted English kitchens.

Fired Earth
www.firedearth.com
Timeless kitchens and bathrooms; also an excellent range of paint colours.

Plain English
+44 (0)1449 774028
www.plainenglishdesign.co.uk
Elegant, simple wooden kitchens for period interiors.

PAINT

Edward Bulmer Natural Paint
+44 (0)1544 388535
www.edwardbulmerpaint.co.uk
Eco-friendly paints developed by architectural historian and interior designer Edward Bulmer.

Farrow & Ball
+44 (0)1202 876141
www.farrow-ball.com
Subtle paint colours with strange names, also papers, primers, and limewash.

Francesca's Paints Ltd
+44 (0)20 7228 7694
www.francescaspaint.com
Traditional limewash, eco-emulsion paint, and chalky emulsion.

Paint & Paper Library
3 Elystan Street
London SW3 3NT
+44 (0)20 7823 7755
www.paintandpaperlibrary.com
Excellent-quality paint, including innumerable shades of off-white.

Papers and Paints
by Patrick Baty
4 Park Walk
London SW10 OAD
+44 (0)20 7352 8626
www.papersandpaints.co.uk
In addition to their own paints, will mix any colour to order.

LIGHTING

John Cullen
561–563 Kings Road
London SW6 2EB
+44 (0)20 7371 9000
www.johncullenlighting.com
Extensive range of light fittings and a bespoke design service.

Pooky
+44 (0)20 7351 3003
www.pooky.com
Excellent online selection of well-priced lighting.

Vaughan
+44 (0)20 7349 4600
www.vaughandesigns.com
Comprehensive range of replica period lighting.

WALLCOVERINGS

Cole & Son Ltd
+44 (0)20 7376 4628
www.cole-and-son.com
Wonderful wallpapers, from the traditional to the wacky.

De Gournay
112 Old Church Street
London SW3 6EP
+44 (0)20 7352 9988
www.degournay.com
Reproductions of hand-painted 18th-century Chinese wallpapers.

Hamilton Weston Wallpapers Ltd.
The Studio
11 Townshend Road
Richmond
Surrey TW9 1XH
+44 (0)20 8940 4850
www.hamiltonweston.com
Historic, bespoke, and original wallpapers, including wonderful designs by contemporary artists Marthe Armitage and Flora Roberts

Zardi and Zardi
Podgwell Barn
Sevenleaze Lane
Edge
Stroud
Gloucestershire GL6 6NJ
+44 (0)1452 814777
www.zardiandzardi.co.uk
Fabulous reproduction tapestries, digitally printed on linen and very convincing.

Picture Credits

All photography by Jan Baldwin except where stated.

Endpapers The home of the writer Ros Byam Shaw; 1 Ph. Christopher Drake; 2–3 Jane Moran's cottage in Sussex; 4 A house in Lincolnshire designed by Lulu Carter Design; 5 above left Jane Moran's cottage in Sussex; 5 below left The London home of Mr and Mrs David Smith, designed by Emma Burns of Sibyl Colefax and John Fowler; 5 below right Ph. Jan Baldwin; 7 Nicolette le Pelley's home in London; 8 above John Martin Robinson's house in Lancashire; 8 below Leslie Geddes-Brown and Hew Stevenson's Suffolk house; 9 Matthew and Miranda Eden's home in Wiltshire; 10 stylist Karen Harrison's home in East Sussex available for photo shoots, call 07734 617639; 11 above right Owner of Westcott Design, Peter Westcott's cottage in Somerset; 11 below left William Palin; 12–13 The family home of Ursula and Toby Falconer; 15 A Georgian terraced house in London, designed by Robert and Josyane Young for Rivière Interiors. www.robertyoungantiques.com; 16 The home of Gavin Waddell; 19 The Dorset home of Edward and Jane Hurst; 20–21 Rose Bamford of Dandy Star's home in Cornwall; 22 Ph. Chris Tubbs/Matthew and Miranda Eden's home in Wiltshire; 23 above The London home of Mr and Mrs David Smith, designed by Emma Burns of Sibyl Colefax and John Fowler; 23 below Ph. Chris Tubbs/Powers house, London; 24 Ph. Chris Tubbs/Hotel Endsleigh; 25 The family home of Ursula and Toby Falconer; 26 above left Francoise Price and Gerry Peachey's cottage in Wiltshire; 26 above right Egford House, the home of Liddie and Howard Holt Harrison; 26 below left stylist Karen Harrison's home in East Sussex available for photo shoots, call 07734 617639; 27 The home of Lucy Bathurst of Nest Design; 28 The home of Iain and Zara Milligan in Scotland; 29 The home of Jack Brister and Richard Nares in Frome, Somerset; 30–31 Ph. Chris Tubbs/Leslie Geddes-Brown and Hew Stevenson's Suffolk house; 31 right Ph. Fritz von der Schulenburg – des. Janet Fitch; 32 Ph. Ben Edwards/The home of Jon and Louise Bunning of Mora Lifestyle; 33 Ph. Simon Brown; 34 above left William Palin; 34 above right Ph. Fritz von der Schulenburg; 34 below left Ph. Simon Brown; 35 Jane Moran's cottage in Sussex; 36 The home of the writer Ros Byam Shaw; 39 The home of the Rt Hon Simon Burns M.P.; 40–41 George Saumarez Smith's home in Winchester; 42 Ph. Chris Tubbs/Leslie Geddes-Brown and Hew Stevenson's Suffolk house; 43 Annabel Lewis Designer; 44 Cressida Granger of Mathmos' cottage in Dorset; 45 above The Suffolk home of Katie Fontana, creative director of Plain English; 45 below right Ph. Ben Edwards/A country cottage in Suffolk, the home of Amanda and Belle Daughtry; 46 Ph. Gavin Kingcome; 47 Egford House, the home of Liddie and Howard Holt Harrison; 48–49 Jo Scofield and Andrew Yarme in Bristol; 50–51 The home of photographer Jan Baldwin; 52 Ph. Simon Brown; 53 Ph. Simon Brown; 54–55 Ph. Simon Brown; 56–57 sophieconran.com, flowers and arrangements by The Blacksmiths Daughter; 58 The London home of Ben Pentreath and Charlie McCormick; 59 Ph. Ben Edwards/The home of Jon and Louise Bunning of Mora Lifestyle; 60 The home of Frank Hollmeyer and Robert Weems; 61 artist Sandra Whitmore's cottage, kitchen by Plain English; 62 The Coleman's family home; 63 Jane Moran's cottage in Sussex; 64 Artist Sandra Whitmore's cottage, kitchen by Plain English; 65 Ph. Chris Tubbs/Matthew and Miranda Eden's home in Wiltshire; 67 Ph. Simon Brown; 68 above Botelet Farm, a special place to stay in Cornwall www.botelet.com; 68 below The Dorset home of Edward and Jane Hurst; 69 Isabel and Julian Bannerman; 70 The home of decorative painter and designer Adam Calkin; 71 above left Ph. Chris Tubbs/Philip and Catherine Mould's house in Oxfordshire; 71 above right The home of decorative painter and designer Adam Calkin; 71 below left Jane Moran's cottage in Sussex; 71 below right Ph. Simon Brown; 72 Artist Binny Mathews and architect Stuart Martin's home in Dorset; 73 Jo Scofield and Andrew Yarme in Bristol; 74 above left The home of the writer Ros Byam Shaw; 74 above right Ph. Chris Tubbs/Leslie Geddes-Brown and Hew Stevenson's Suffolk house; 74 below left Jane Moran's cottage in Sussex; 75 Garden Designer Arne Maynard and William Collinson's home in Monmouthshire; 76 The home of gardener Todd Longstaffe-Gowan and museum director Tim Knox; 77 above left The home of Eva Johnson in Suffolk; 77 above right Caddy and Chris Wilmot-Sitwell's house in Dorset; 77 below right A Charles II Period London Townhouse designed by Robert and Josyane Young of Rivière Interiors; 78–79 Charlotte Molesworth, artist, gardener and flower arranger, cottage in Weald of Kent; 80 Ph. Simon Brown; 81 above Ph. Simon Brown; 81 below The home of Doris Urquhart and Christopher Richardson, antique dealers in Suffolk; 83 Ph. Simon Brown; 84 Ph. Christopher Drake; 85 above The home of Doris Urquhart and Christopher Richardson, antique dealers in Suffolk; 85 below Ph. Simon Brown; 86 A house in the West Country designed by its owners and Emma Sims-Hilditch www.simshilditch.com; 87 The home of Maria and Frank in Southern Germany, with interior design by Barbara Gügel; 89 above Egford House, the home of Liddie and Howard Holt Harrison; 89 below The home of Eva Johnson in Suffolk; 90 Herrington House in Dorset, the home of Raymond and Pollyann Williams; 91 Ph. Simon Brown; 92 Ph. Simon Brown; 93 The London home of Lulu Lytle of Soane Britain; 95 Ben Pentreath's first Dorset home, the West Wing at Bellamont; 96 Ph. Jan Baldwin; 98–99 Ph. Jan Baldwin; 100 Ph. Simon Brown; 101 The family home of Bill and Becca Collison in Sussex; 102 Ph. Gavin Kingcome; 103 Ph. Jan Baldwin; 104–105 Chris Dyson Architects; 106 Ph. Simon Brown; 107 Ph. James Merrell/decorated by Roger Banks-Pye of Colefax & Fowler; 108 above Francoise Price and Gerry Peachey's cottage in Wiltshire; 108 below Ph. Fritz von der Schulenburg –des. Jill de Brand; 109 Ph. Gavin Kingcome; 110–111 Artist Binny Mathews and architect Stuart Martin's home in Dorset; 112 Ph. Simon Brown; 113 A Charles II Period London Townhouse designed by Robert and Josyane Young of Riviere Interiors; 114 above Ph. Chris Tubbs/Julia and Michael Pruskin's family home; 114 below left Ph. Fritz von der Schulenburg – des. Willa Elphinstone; 114 below right Ph. Fritz von der Schulenburg –des. Janet Fitch; 115 Ph. Jan Baldwin; 116 above Ph. Simon Brown; 116 below Ph. Gavin Kingcome; 117 Ph. Gavin Kingcome; 118 A house in the West Country designed by its owners and Emma Sims-Hilditch www.simshilditch.com; 119 Ph. Chris Tubbs/Powers house, London; 121 The home of Jack Brister and Richard Nares in Frome, Somerset; 122 Ph. Chris Tubbs/Justin and Eliza Meath-Baker's house in the West Country; 124–125 carpentry and joinery by Martin Brown, painting by Taylors Interiors Ltd; 125 above right Ph. Simon Brown; 125 below right Ph. Simon Upton; 126 The home of Frank Hollmeyer and Robert Weems; 127 A house in the West Country designed by its owners and Emma Sims-Hilditch www.simshilditch.com; 128 left The London home of Conrad Roeber and David Townsend of Schubert Masters design practice; 128–129 A house in Norfolk designed by George Carter, paint effects by Paola Cumiskey; 130 Architect William Smalley's London flat; 131 above left Designer Helen Ellery's home in London; 131 above right Ph. Gavin Kingcome; 131 below right Ph. Ben Edwards/Lucy Haywood's home in the country; 132 above Ph. Fritz von der Schulenburg; 132 below William Palin; 133 Ph. Gavin Kingcome; 135 Ph. Simon Brown; 136 Ph. Simon Brown; 138–139 Ph. Gavin Kingcome; 140 Ph. Simon Brown; 141 Ph. Simon Brown; 142 above left Ph. Simon Brown; 142 above right Ph. Simon Brown; 142 below left Melanie Molesworth, freelance interiors stylist; 143 The Temple, home of Veere Grenney; 144 Ph. Christopher Drake; 145 Ph. Christopher Drake; 146 Folliots Farmhouse, the home of the ceramicist Patricia Low and an artist's retreat in Hampshire; 147 Ph. James Merrell/decorated by Roger Banks-Pye of Colefax & Fowler; 148 The home of Lori and William

Index

Gibson; 149 above right Ph. Jan Baldwin; 149 below left Designer
Helen Ellery's home in London; 149 below right Ph. Tim Beddow;
150 above The Dorset home of Ben Pentreath and Charlie
McCormick; 150 below Ph. Chris Tubbs/Elizabeth Baer's early
Georgian home; 151 Ph. Jan Baldwin; 152 Jane Moran's cottage
in Sussex; 153 Ph. Chris Tubbs/John Martin Robinson's house
in Lancashire; 154 Artist Sandra Whitmore's cottage, kitchen by
Plain English; 155 above The home of the writer Ros Byam Shaw;
155 below Ph. Fritz von der Schulenburg; 157 The home of Jack
Brister and Richard Nares in Frome, Somerset; 158 The home
of Lucy Bathurst of Nest Design; 160 Folliots Farmhouse, the
home of the ceramicist Patricia Low and an artist's retreat in
Hampshire; 161 above left The family home of Bill and Becca
Collison in Sussex; 161 above right Ph. Simon Brown; 161
below left Ph. Ben Edwards/The London home of Emma Gurmin
(@velvetribbon.home); 161 below right Ph. Chris Tubbs/Matthew
and Mairanda Eden's home in Wiltshire; 162–163 The home of
textile designer Richard Smith and art dealer Andrew Blackman;
164 The family home of Ursula and Toby Falconer; 165 above
left The home of the writer Ros Byam Shaw; 165 above right
Ph. Chris Tubbs/ Designer Emily Todhunter's holiday home in
the Peak District; 165 below Ph. Jan Baldwin/George Carter's
cottage in Norfolk; 166 The home of Gavin Waddell; 167 Ph.
Simon Brown; 168 left The home of Jack Brister and Richard
Nares in Frome, Somerset; 168–169 Ph. Christopher Drake;
171 The Dorset home of Edward and Jane Hurst; 172 above right
Ph. Christopher Drake; 172 below left Artist Binny Mathews
and architect Stuart Martin's home in Dorset; 172 below right
The Walled Garden at Cowdray; 173 The Dorset home of Ben
Pentreath and Charlie McCormick; 174 Ph. Simon Brown; 175 Ph.
Simon Brown; 176 above left Kristin Krogstad Interior Architect,
www.thedrawingroom.no; 176 below left William Palin; 176
below right A house in Norfolk deigned by George Carter, paint
effects by Paola Cumiskey; 177 The home of decorative painter
and designer Adam Calkin; 178 Ph. Simon Brown; 179 Ph.
Christopher Drake; 180 Ph. Simon Brown; 181 A house in Norfolk
deigned by George Carter, paint effects by Paola Cumiskey; 182
The home of Sophie Lambert, owner of Au Temps des Cerises
in France; 183 above Ph. Chris Tubbs/The home of the writer
Ros Byam Shaw; 183 below Ph. Jan Baldwin; 184 William Palin;
185 above John Nicholson's house is available as a film and
photographic location; 185 below and 186 Ph. Gavin Kingcome;
188 The home of the writer Ros Byam Shaw; 189 The Suffolk
home of Katie Fontana, creative director of Plain English; 190
Ph. Chris Tubbs/ Annabel Grey's Norfolk cottage; 191 Ph. Simon
Brown; 192 The Dorset home of Edward and Jane Hurst; 193
above left The home of Jack Brister and Richard Nares in Frome,
Somerset; 193 above right Owner of Westcott Design, Peter
Westcott's cottage in Somerset; 193 below right The home of
Anita Evagora and David Campbell; 194–195 The home of gardener
Todd Longstaffe-Gowan and museum director Tim Knox; 196
above Ph.Chris Tubbs/Nicolette le Pelley's home in London;
196 below The home of the writer Ros Byam Shaw; 197 Melanie
Molesworth, freelance interiors stylist; 198 above left The home
of Frank Hollmeyer and Robert Weems; 198 above right The Reilly
family in Deal, Kent; 198 below left Ph. Fritz von der Schulenburg
– des. John Russell; 198 below right Ph. Simon Brown; 199
above left The home of Matt and Jax Fothergill in Shropshire;
199 above right Ph. Chris Tubbs/Annabel Grey's Norfolk cottage;
199 below right Sue and David Gentleman's house in London;
202 A Charles II Period London Townhouse designed by Robert
and Josyane Young of Rivière Interiors; 206–207 Garsington
Manor, home of Mrs Rosalind Ingrams and her family.

Page numbers in *italic* refer
to the illustrations

A
Agas 36, 37, 38, 40–2, 55, 59,
  65
airing/hot cupboards 82
antiques 120–3, 121–33
armchairs 37, 94, 95, 102–3,
  109, 113, 119, 123, 148
auctions 120, 123

B
back doors 17
Baldwin, Jan 38
basement kitchens 37, 50–1, 60
baskets 18, 24, 33, 43, 88
bathrooms 134, 170, 171–85
bathtubs 170, 171–3, 175–6,
  178, 180, 184
bed linen 137
bedrooms 67, 134–7, 135–55
bedspreads 137, 159, 161, 164–5
Belfast sinks 82
benches, in halls 18, 24, 26
Bennison, Geoffrey 156
blinds 159
book rests 125
bookshelves 35, 117, 149,
  151–2, 187, 196
boot rooms 82, 88, 91
Bowood House, Wiltshire 156
box beds 146
brick floors 45, 60, 85
butcher's blocks 44
butler's pantries 82

C
cabinets, display 187, 193
Calkin, Adam 70, 177
carpets
  bathrooms 178
  bedrooms 137
  runners 34
  on stairs 28, 34
  see also rugs
chairs 38, 120, 122, 125, 126
chalk paint 77
chandeliers 132
chests-of-drawers 120, 137, 155,
  170
children's rooms 137
china 128
  collections 186, 187, 188, 190
  antique china 131, 133
  Cornishware 39, 187
chintz 97, 134, 141, 145, 153,
  156, 157, 159, 160–1, 168
Cliveden 134
cloakrooms 82, 176
clocks 18, 28, 193
clothes, storage 137, 142
coat hooks 17, 24, 26–7, 142

coffee tables 103, 108
coir mats 32
collections 39, 97, 186, 187,
  188–99
colours
  bedrooms 137, 149
  living rooms 97
Cornishware 39, 187
coronas 134, 145
cotton fabrics 137, 156
Crosland, Neisha 50–1
cupboards
  clothes storage 137
  curtains 38, 50, 93
  in kitchens 36, 38, 40–1
  larders 86
  pantries 87
curtains 156, 158, 159, 161–3,
  168–9
  in bedrooms 134, 137, 141
  kitchen cupboards 38, 50, 93
  in kitchens 46
cushions 75, 98–100, 112, 142,
  156, 160, 165

D
dealers, antiques 123
desks 125
dining chairs 120
dining tables 18, 128–9
dishwashers 82, 85
displays see collections
distemper 42, 74, 77
doors, halls 17
'drab' paintwork 76
draining boards 82
drawing rooms see living rooms
dressers 37, 121, 186, 187, 188
duvet covers 137

E F
Ede, Jim 197
English Country House style 37,
  66
entrance halls 16, 17–18, 19–35
Ercol 120

fabrics 156–9, 157–69
  antique 127
  in bedrooms 134–7, 135, 142,
    144–7
  in living rooms 97, 112, 116
  patina 66, 69, 75
farmhouse kitchens 37, 72
Farrow & Ball 23
fireplaces 94, 95, 97, 101–8,
  111, 116
fitted kitchens 37, 38, 62
flagstones 17, 68, 83
flats
  halls 17, 23
  kitchens 58, 73
  utility rooms 93

flooring
  brick *45, 60, 85*
  in halls 17, *19*
  painted floors *26, 58, 172*
  slate floors *68*
  stone floors 17, 66, *68, 72, 83*
  tiled floors *61*
  wooden floors *22, 62, 67, 73, 77, 81, 154*
flowers 97, *114*, 156
Formica 37
four-poster beds 134, *136, 144, 150, 153*
Fowler, John 66, 156
front doors 17
furniture
  antiques 120–3, *121–33*
  in halls 18
  in kitchens 37, *54*
  in living rooms 97
  patina 66

G H
galley kitchens *58*
glassware, collections 187

half-tester beds 134, *168*
halls *16*, 17–18, *19–35*
Hampton Court 156
Henry VIII, King 156
home offices *125*

I K
inglenook fireplaces 94, *116*
islands, kitchen *56–7*

Kettle's Yard, Cambridge *197*
Kime, Robert 94
kitchens *36*, 37–8, *38–65*

L
lampshades *135, 138, 149, 168*
Lancaster, Nancy 66, 94–7, 134, 170
landings *26, 34*
larders *64*, 82, *86, 89–90*
laundry rooms 82, *85, 93*
lavatories 170, *176–7*
leather, patina *71*
Lewis & Wood *25*
libraries *128–9*
lighting
  antique *132*
  in bedrooms 137
  in halls *33*
  in kitchens 38
  in utility rooms *115–16*
lime plaster 66, *71, 74*
limewash *45, 68, 74–5, 78–9*
linen, bed 137
living rooms 94–7, *95–119*
loose covers/slipcovers *114*, 156

M
materials, patina 66, *67–81*
matting *32, 150*
mirrors 66, *71*
  in bathrooms 170, *180*
  collections 187, *198*
  in halls 18
  in living rooms *107*
  patina *80*
Mughal art 156
murals *70*

N O
Nest Design *158*

offices *125*
ornaments 97
ottomans *103*, 156

P
paint
  chalk paint *77*
  distemper *42, 74, 77*
  'drab' paintwork *76*
  floors *26, 58, 172*
  in kitchens *36, 42*
  limewash *45, 68, 74–5, 78–9*
  patina 66, *77*
panelling *34, 71, 76, 80, 100, 113, 117, 132, 155, 176*
pantries 82, *87*
patchwork 134, *150, 154*, 159
patina 66, *67–81*
photographs 187, *191*
pianos 18, *20–1, 34–5*
pictures
  antiques *124–5, 131*
  in bathrooms *181*
  collections 187, *196, 198*
  in halls 18, *23, 31, 33*
  in kitchens 37
  in living rooms 94, *96, 116*
pillowcases 137
plaster 66, *71, 73, 74*
plate racks 38
pot plants 97, *173*

Q R
quarry tiles *63*

range cookers *36*, 37, 38, *40–2, 55, 59, 65*
Rivière Interiors *77*
rugs *165*
  in halls 17
  in living rooms 94, *112, 114*
  see also carpets
runners *34*

S
sanitary ware 170
scale, living rooms 97
sculleries 82, *85*

'shabby chic' 66
sheets 137, 159
shelves
  bookshelves *117, 149, 151–2, 187, 196*
  in kitchens 38, *47, 65*
  in larders *89–90*
  in utility rooms 82
shoes 17–18, *26*
showers 170
side tables *106, 108, 114*
sinks 82, *89*
sitting rooms *see* living rooms
slate
  floors *68*
  shelves 82
  sinks *89*
  work surfaces *89*
slipcovers/loose covers *114*, 156
sofas 94, *95–6, 98–101, 105–6, 110, 114–15, 118*, 123
Spode 187
staircases 16, 17, *20–3, 26, 28–9, 31, 34–5*
stone floors 17, 66, *68, 72, 83*

T
tables
  antique *128, 130*
  coffee tables *103, 108*
  dining tables 18, *128–9*
  kitchen tables 37, *46, 48–9, 51–3, 56, 64*, 120
  side tables *106, 108, 114*
tallboys *126*
tapestries 159
televisions 97

terraced houses 17
terracotta 17, 38, *62*
throws *108–9, 140*
tiles
  bathrooms *176*
  floors 17, *19, 61, 63*
towels *182*
townhouses 17, *48–52, 103*

U V
unfitted kitchens 37, *44–5, 47, 54*
upholstery 123, 156
utility rooms 82, *83–93*

Victorian houses 82
vintage 120

W
wallpaper
  in bathrooms *172, 183, 185*
  in bedrooms 137
  in halls *16, 23, 25*
  in kitchens *53*
  in living rooms 97
wardrobes 137
washbasins 170, *180*
washing machines 82, *85*
Wedgwood 187
wine cellars *85*
wood
  fitted kitchens 37
  floors *22, 62, 67, 73, 77, 81, 154*
  panelling *34, 71, 76, 80, 100, 113, 117, 132, 155, 176*
  patina 66
work surfaces *44–5, 68, 89*

Acknowledgments

This book was written during the Covid-19 pandemic. It was an ideal lockdown project, being illustrated with images from the photographic library of Ryland Peters & Small and its sister company CICO Books, and the first person I should thank is Publishing Director Cindy Richards. It was her idea to create this compendium of the *Perfect English* series, and I am grateful for her inspiration, enthusiasm and support, and for that of Art Director Leslie Harrington. Annabel Morgan worked her magic as editor and is always a pleasure to collaborate with, and Toni Kay came up with an elegant design that unites pictures taken by a variety of photographers over a number of years. Isabel de Cordova was a great help with the picture research. This book is more than a summation of a style; it is a coming together of the ideas – and contacts – of other authors, the talent of photographers, and the creativity of the designers and house owners whose rooms are shown here. I am indebted to all of them.

Perfect English Quotes

When I first started this book, and was trying to crystallize the most abiding characteristics of English decoration, I decided to ask the people who follow me on Instagram for their thoughts. I wasn't expecting such a tremendous response. I wish I had space to quote more of the hundreds of witty, perceptive things that were said, but here are a few. I kept their authors anonymous – but you know who you are …

'always mending, mending …'

'a love of things from the past, valued for their colour, pattern, and quality'

'prouder of a charity shop or jumble sale find than a solid, inherited piece'

'cobwebs are a must!'

'burning fronts and freezing backs in front of the fire in winter sitting rooms'

'perfectly imperfect, with soul'

'artlessness, or at least the impression of artlessness'

'pelargoniums, a well-stocked drinks tray, inherited paintings that you wouldn't choose'

'affection for belongings overriding fashion'

'toast racks, butter dishes, and teapots; a roaring open fire; persistent draughts; long shadows and the Aga'

'eccentricity, originality, inevitability, permanence'

'a bit too much of everything for regular dusting'

'a deep sense of heritage, an overall nonchalance, and an absence of dogma about colour or matching'

'an overall unpretentious mix of beautiful, gently aged objects'

'the evidence of history everywhere you look, and the confident "as you find us" attitude'

'a flow from house to garden'

'like the best of English manners, the purpose is not to impress or intimidate, but to comfort and set the mind at ease'

'a well-considered disregard for rules, and an often brave expression of oneself'

'a gentle layering of generations'

'reimagining the past through rose-tinted spectacles'

'big sofas, big dogs, big roses in silver bowls, big cow parsley, big drinks'

'the keynote is not display but ease'

'a sense that visitors are welcome and can be comfortable – no worries about sitting on the wrong chair or feeling bad if you have brought a bit of mud in on your boots'

'a willingness to let the outside in – not only in fabric, prints, and paintings, but wisteria coming in through the bathroom window'

'an acceptance of the fact that you can't control everything and that a house is never truly just yours'

'wonky lampshades'

'gardens seen through doorways and a certain generosity in everything'

'domesticated nature gently woven through every ordinary thing'

'a great sense of belonging and tradition, timelessness and seasonal awareness, and above all of sanctuary'

'never looks as though a professional decorator has been involved, but as though it has just evolved over time, with imperfections but much warmth and charm'

'good and bad paintings, enormous jugs of garden flowers, lots of books, wellington boots, sudden unexpected exotica and brilliant colour clashes, good old cutlery, old radios, slightly mad wallpaper'

'nothing too precise, or too fussy, and the comfort of cushioned sound'

'soft, weathered, cosy, sturdy, generous, unaffected, and blissfully indifferent to "taste"'

'busy – nothing too new and shiny'

'looks unconsidered, but almost certainly isn't – more about appearing not to be trying too hard'

'indoor geraniums, worn out chintz, floppy cushions, loose covers, "making do", kitchen suppers, a little bit of dust, ashes in fireplaces, dogs, Agas, and plain, honest cabinetry'

'designed to please the owner – impervious to trends – with a sense of wit, and a dash of eccentricity'

'resourcefulness, thrift, and tolerance'